The
Gift
of
Love

The
Gift
of
Love

Compiled by the Editors of Guideposts Books

Illustrations by Jo Haight

GUIDEPOSTS®
Carmel, NY 10512

The Gift of Love

Contents

Contents

The Gift of Love

Introduction

Make love your aim! Here at Guideposts that is one of the biblical commands we work hard to fulfill, and it is the underlying foundation of what we do and the stories we publish. How can we show love in action?

Jesus told us that love is the first, the highest commandment—to love God with everything we are. Love is the second commandment—to love our neighbor as we love ourselves. And then He gave us a new commandment, a new standard by which to judge and measure love. We are to love in the same way He has loved us (John 15:12).

Such love may seem impossible, but that's why Paul told us to make love our aim (1 Corinthians 14:1, RSV). We are to keep trying, knowing that every time we put love into action, in however small a way, we are proving that we belong to Christ (John 13:35), and so are changing our world.

And how do we love like that? In *The Gift of Love* you'll find more than seventy illustrations of or comments on Jesus' kind of love. Love that thinks of others and puts them first. Love that acts, not primarily with grandiose gestures or expensive gifts, but in almost unnoticed actions, in encouraging words spoken at the right time. Love that does the loving thing, regardless of feelings. Love that gives—and for-gives—and so works to transform situations, enemies, even ourselves.

We invite you to celebrate the power and beauty of love,

not only in the pages of *The Gift of Love* but also by putting
it into practice in your own life.
Become a lover in deed!

—The Editors

PART 1

Giving Love a Chance

Before you can give love, you have to give it a chance in your own life. Like the young mother with a bothersome neighbor, the marriage counselor with a critical wife, and the fearful mother with a premature baby, you too can discover that opening the door to love—even just a crack—will give you a joyful new life in which love blossoms.

A Sprig of Understanding
Faye Field

THE ALTHEA BUSH is my favorite of all the plants in our yard. When it blooms in July, its white blossoms—delicate as orchids with their circles of mauve—seem to be cushioned on its rich dark-green leaves. I often catch myself gazing out the window, drinking in the beauty of the plant with its old-fashioned look of grace and remembering how it came to me so many Christmases ago.

During World War II, when my husband was in the Navy, I went back to Mother with my newborn baby. Mama lived in a little east Texas village, population 232. The social life here consisted of neighbors borrowing from one another and staying to chat a spell on the porch or in the kitchen.

Little Michael had colic and required many hours of careful tending. As soon as I got him bathed and fed and he finally dropped off for a morning nap, I would begin writing my daily letter to my husband. In fact, this was the only time I had for this respite.

Every day, just as I sat down at the kitchen table to begin, in would come Mrs. Manly. How I resented this daily intrusion! She was always slightly out of breath, even though she had only walked across the garden lot that separated her place from Mama's. She plopped in the cane-bottom chair next to the table.

Each day it was the same. She smoothed out her checked apron slowly and carefully in her lap. She brushed long, stray strands of brownish-gray hair back from each temple, tucking them snugly behind her ears. Then she'd look over and touch the old blue stoneware pitcher she had placed on the edge of the table.

"Here's my pitcher. I need some buttermilk." She reached deep in her apron pocket for her nickel. She looked at it longingly as she reluctantly gave it to Mama for the gallon of creamy buttermilk.

Each day I'd sit back in my chair, silently hoping that she would be on her way, but no, she'd start talking endlessly. Mama was never much of a talker. Mrs. Manly rambled on mostly about her visits to the doctor. She suffered from a malady in which she "had too much blood." The doctor had to "bleed her." She spared no grisly details. Morning after morning I listened to her tales of woe, and I began to loathe her droning complaints. Mama's house was so small that there was no escaping her, and I cringed in fear that her constant chatter would waken the baby.

One day about two weeks before Christmas, just after Mrs. Manly left from her daily visit, I burst out to Mama, "Oh, that woman! She's driving me crazy. All she cares about is herself."

Mama gave me a long look. Finally she said, "Oh, I don't know about that, Faye. Maybe you haven't given Mrs. Manly a chance to love you."

"How can that be?" I exclaimed.

"Maybe Mrs. Manly's just talking to fill in our silences," Mama said. Well, that was true. I'd been so bored and anxious for her to make her visits short that about all I ever said to her was "um."

I went to my bedroom and prayed. *Lord, clean my heart and mind, and make me ready for this blessed time of Your birth* . . . Somehow as I prayed, I kept seeing Mrs. Manly's plain old face rising about my bedstead, popping up in the corner where the diaper pail stood, appearing out of the embers in the fireplace. Surely the Lord was trying to tell me something about my neighbor.

Maybe Mama was right. I hadn't really given Mrs. Manly a chance to love me. How can you love someone who groans at the sight of you? So the next morning when she came to our door, I rushed to open it for her and greeted her enthusiastically. She looked startled, but she smiled.

When I asked her how she soothed a colicky baby, Mrs. Manly beamed (and later I found that her advice helped). Within ten minutes, Mrs. Manly and I were swapping stories and she was telling me about a fascinating adventure she'd had with her husband.

When she left, I no longer felt bored and put upon, but rather warm and happy inside. I actually began to look forward to Mrs. Manly's visits.

Then came Christmas Eve. When Mrs. Manly arrived on the morning of that day, she was carrying two small cellophane wrappings along with her blue stoneware pitcher. She gave one to Mama and one to me. However, she spoke directly to me.

"I'm too poor to buy you anything for Christmas. I used to crochet gifts, but now my eyes won't permit me to do that. I wanted to give you something, because you have been so much company to me every morning. So I rooted this althea sprig for you. You always thought it had such pretty flowers. It's easy to grow. When your husband gets out of the Navy and you get settled, maybe you'd like to plant it in your own yard."

I could feel my cheeks flush with gratitude and shame at the same time. With one hand I took the althea sprig, and with my other I patted Mrs. Manly's rough face, now quite lovely to me in its warm glow of giving. "Thank you, thank you!" I said. "You've been so nice to me these past weeks." And I meant it.

That's how I came to have a glorious nine-foot althea bush in our front yard. And it's how I learned something valuable about neighborliness. As Mama said, give the other person a chance to love *you*.

Before You Can
Love Someone
Odell McBrayer

BEFORE I LEFT HOME for my law office this morning, I paused in front of the bedroom mirror and spoke to myself. It took no more than ten seconds, but they are seconds that have transformed my marriage and scores of others I encounter in my daily practice.

I'd never wanted to handle divorce cases, but by the 1970s they made up a staggering sixty percent of my work—and from what I read in law journals, that figure was not unusual. It staggered not only my mind, but also my conscience. As a Christian I believed there were no successful divorce cases, that divorce was never the answer. And yet, what other answer was there for such widespread unhappiness?

Thus I'd gone back for special training, hoping to find ways to help my clients. And the advice I was taught to give was doubtless good: To get love, give love. Be appreciative. To the women, "Try a new hairdo." To the husbands, "Buy your wife some flowers."

The results I got with the training were the same as before—almost none. But I tried not to let myself worry about it. I had no time to worry. President of the Junior Chamber of Commerce, member of the school board, treasurer of the church, I'd also decided in 1974 to run in the Republican primary for governor of Texas.

If all this meant very little time with my wife, Nelda, well, the fact was I was growing tired of her endless criticism and faultfinding. The last time I'd taken her out to dinner, for example, instead of being pleased, she'd complained because five or six campaign workers came along. Or take our vacation the previous summer. I'd taken Nelda and our two kids to a church conference in a beautiful hotel right beside a lake, and all she said was, "Why can't we ever go anywhere just as a family?"

For all the while I was counseling others about their marriages, I was blind to the mammoth problems in my own. Why didn't I spot them sooner? All the symptoms were there. The increasingly bitter quarrels about the committees and meetings that kept me away from home. Our inability to discuss anything without turning it into an argument.

Maybe the trouble was that the marriages I dealt with at the office so often involved husbands who drank or fooled around or failed to support their families. I was a prominent citizen, a pillar of the church, an adviser to the National Alliance for Family Life! My marriage couldn't be as bad as theirs.

So why, one evening when I got home from a Sunday school teachers' meeting, did I find Nelda marking the apartments-for-rent column in the local paper?

"It's what you want, isn't it?" she said quietly. "For me to move out." I was stunned. I just didn't believe it. For Nelda to leave me? At last, by promising to start going together to the Fort Worth Family Counseling Service (of which I, ironically, was director), I persuaded her to postpone her decision.

And the counseling helped—some. We learned to communicate, anyway, to talk to each other. And yet somehow we never seemed to get at the basic problem.

It was one of my clients who gave me the clue. She'd tried, she said, really tried to show love and appreciation and all the other things I'd recommended, but her husband had not responded. "You see, he never should have married me in the first place. He's popular and I've never been. I'm no good at meeting people. I can't learn languages like he can and . . ."

Why, I thought suddenly, *it isn't only her husband who's rejecting her.*

This woman can't stand herself. And then on the heels of that thought, like a flash of lightning, came another one! *Is it possible that lack of self-appreciation is at the bottom of my own marital troubles?*

Angrily I tried to push the thought aside. I was Odell McBrayer, a successful lawyer, wasn't I? I was a leader in the community. I was . . .

"Wait a minute," said a quiet voice somewhere inside of me. "Think back . . ."

I thought back to my childhood, trying to remember a single time when someone had kissed me or even put an arm around me. On our small cotton farm in the 1930s there hadn't been time for the luxury of love. My earliest memory, at the age of four, was of the cotton sack across my shoulder growing heavier and heavier as I dragged it down the endless rows.

Later I remember plowing behind a team of horses in the spring. Planting under the Texas summer sun. Leaving school to pull cotton in the fall. Dad expected my sister and me to get as much in our two sacks as he put in his one—and Dad was a human cotton-pulling machine. I felt like I could never work fast enough or well enough for him.

And it wasn't only Dad I felt I couldn't satisfy. I saw again the lighted Christmas tree outside our little crossroads filling station. Underneath that tree each year would be heaped the riches of heaven itself—football, skates, little toy cars. One by one, as each name was called, the children of the neighborhood would step forward to receive their gifts. I never reasoned out that the various families had bought those gifts and placed them there, and that some families—like mine—couldn't afford any. It seemed to me that the bright packages really had dropped from heaven, and as year after year my name was never called, it was clear that God Himself was displeased with me.

Then in May 1974, when I was defeated in the Republican primary, wasn't it true that my reaction had been much more intense than was normal? Hadn't I felt that it was not just the voters but the whole world that had rejected me?

Now, still hurting from the defeat, I could see that this feeling of not being good enough went very deep. It wasn't as though I hadn't tried to make myself good enough. I saw myself getting out of the Air Force and enrolling in night school. Doing five years of college work in three. Working fifteen to eighteen hours a day to support Nelda and the babies. Succeed! Make it! Get out of the cotton fields! That was what my conscious mind told me.

And yet all the while, deep inside, a nagging inner voice was whispering, "Not good enough."

Suddenly I saw all the "worthwhile" things I did, all my committees, surrounding myself with people—even on vacation—as a desperate attempt to drown out that voice. Was I so very different from men who tried to drown self-loathing in a bottle or a love affair? Wasn't every one of us, deep-down, trying to escape from himself?

That was the trouble with all those methods—they didn't work. No matter how many titles and positions I accumulated—supposing even I'd become governor of Texas—would it make any difference in the way I felt about myself?

Now, at last, knowing that I needed help, I turned to the book where I'd found help before—the Bible. I started at the beginning. There, in the very first chapter, I read that God looked around at what He had made and, behold, *everything*—not just some of it—was very good.

Later in the same book, sin enters the world. Toil, failure, unhappiness—those were the passages I'd always identified with. But I turned to the New Testament and read that God wiped all of that out when Jesus died—that He put everything back exactly as it was in the beginning when it was good and new and wonderful. I read the commandment I'd heard every Sunday: "Thou shalt love the Lord thy God with all thy heart, and with all thy soul . . . and with all thy mind; and thy neighbor as thyself" (Luke 10:27).

Up until that moment I would have said I was trying to live by it. Wasn't I serving God as well as I knew how? Wasn't I trying to be a good neighbor?

But in that instant I realized I'd overlooked something. One little word.

Thyself.

Slowly I crossed the bedroom to the mirror over the dresser. My own hangdog countenance gazed out at me.

Do you love that man there? God seemed to be asking me.

Of course I didn't! I knew that man too well to love him. Why he . . .

Why not? God's voice persisted. *I do. I made him, I died for him.*

"But, Lord Jesus, if You knew all the vile, ugly things that man has . . . " And then I realized I was talking to the one Person who did know.

I'm not asking you what kind of man he is, He seemed to say. *I love him because it is My nature to love, freely and unconditionally, and I will not permit you to despise what I love.*

It took a long while, standing there in front of the mirror. I got it out at last, "God loves you." And, then, harder still, "And I love you," to the guy who looked so doubtfully back at me.

I did it again the next day. And the next.

And by a curious coincidence, at the same time Nelda was growing less critical. Days would go by and she wouldn't have a negative thing to say. At last I commented on the change in her. Her blue eyes searched my face. "Odell, I haven't changed. You're the one who's different. You used to take every little thing I said as some kind of attack. Lately you've been so much easier to live with!"

Was it possible? For twenty-five years could I have been reading into Nelda's words and actions simply my own low opinion of myself? Sure enough, as the weeks passed and each morning I opened myself a little more to the Holy Spirit's love, I began to be more aware of Nelda's love, too. Of my children's love. My friends' love. The slights, the hurts, the disapproval—when I stopped expecting them, they largely stopped happening!

I began to share my discovery with my clients. To every "unappreciated" husband or wife I gave the same directions: Read the first chapter of Genesis. Ask God to forgive you for failing to love and esteem His perfect creation in yourself. Accept His forgiveness. Then stand in front of the mirror and say, "God loves you and I love you!"

It may sound foolish and simplistic. I only know I used to have virtually no success in reconciling unhappy couples, and that now well over 50 percent of the people who come to me for divorces stay married and report a better relationship than they've ever known. Oh, I still give the recommended advice. I still urge husbands and wives to be more demonstrative, to show approval, to try a little praise. But I remind them not to leave the person who may need it most — the one looking back out of the mirror.

A Message from God
Daniel Schantz

WHENEVER I BACK out of my driveway, the words *I LOVE YOU* appear in the rear window of my car in bold, white letters. Actually, the words are chalked on the back of our neighbor's brick garage. A teen-aged girl put them there, hoping her boyfriend would see them on his walk home from school.

Most of the time I don't even notice the words, but sometimes they seem to glow like a message from God, written with an angel's hand.

When I am depressed, the message is "I LOVE YOU."

When I am angry, the message reads, "I LOVE YOU."

When I am torn with guilt, the words are "I LOVE YOU."

When I am terrified of the future, He whispers, "I LOVE YOU."

Those three words have taught me a lesson about the unconditional love of God. No, God does not love all the things I do, and He would like me to change. But *always* He *loves me*, no matter what.

I love you. The chalky words are growing dim from recent rains and I plan to renew them. Perhaps you would like to write those words on a card and post them where you will see them every day and be reminded that God loves you no matter what your mood or deeds.

1 Pound 9 Ounces
Sandy Garredo

AT LAST the nurse gave in to my desperate questions. "She weighs one pound nine ounces," she said.

The probing lights of the delivery room blurred over my head as unconsciousness stole over me. When I awakened, I was back in my room. My husband, Barry, stepped quickly to my bedside. "Sandy, I called the church. They're praying and they've got a prayer chain going . . ."

I shook my head to cut him off. "Tell me the truth about the baby," I said. "Tell me everything."

A distant look came over Barry's face as he tried to separate his emotions from the medical facts he'd been bombarded with. "The doctor talked to me," he began. "The doctor gives her a twenty percent chance of living. Even if she makes it, she'll probably have brain damage, be blind and have all kinds of other problems. The doctor says she's just too small . . ."

Barry spoke flatly. He stared at the wall as he began to repeat himself. "The doctor says the chances are slim she'll live and even slimmer that she'll be normal if she does live." He turned to me uncertainly. "Sandy . . . do . . . don't you want to see her now?"

I closed my eyes and formed the word "no." *Better not,* said my anxious, tired brain. *Don't get attached. Just rest.*

But I slept fitfully. When the nurses caught me awake, they kept asking if I wanted to see her. It had been twenty-four hours now and I still hadn't seen . . . Kara. Kara was the name we'd picked for a girl. She was Kara, not "it." And she was three months premature.

I thought back to what my obstetrician had told me when I'd begun dilating at only five months. "It all depends," he said carefully, "on how long we can keep from delivering that baby. Chances of survival are fair if we can make it to seven months and if the baby weighs at least two-and-a-half pounds."

Then, only a month later, the contractions began. In spite of surgery and medication—and prayers—the baby was coming far, far too soon. I had pleaded with the Lord that this would not happen. I believed in prayer, and our church was very strong in prayer. But now I felt so frightened it was hard even to pray.

Barry came quietly into the room and sat down beside my bed, taking my hand. "I've been to see her," he said.

I was mute, questioning him with my eyes. "Tiny," he said softly, "so tiny. She's red as a rose and just thirteen inches long. She's in something called an isolette—it's like a small greenhouse for premature babies—and they've got a kind of little cellophane cap on her head to help retain body heat."

"Is she any . . . stronger?" I asked.

Barry looked away. "Well, she's down to one-pound-six," he answered, "but they say a weight loss is normal right after birth."

I gripped Barry's hand. He was working so hard at being brave. But

I was more afraid than he was. Still, I was being selfish. I shouldn't allow my fear to weigh him down. "I — I'll go see her now," I said in a trembly voice.

The tires of my wheelchair turned rhythmically as Barry pushed it toward the ICU nursery—*one pound six ounces, one pound six ounces, one pound six ounces* . . .

We passed the viewing windows of the nursery. Each isolette had its own thicket of tubes and respirators, pumps and monitors for heartbeat and breathing. Alert to each set of beeps and flashing lights, the nurses worked one-on-one, guarding each little life.

A nurse showed us where to wash our hands and put on the sterile gowns she'd given us. Finally we were beside our baby's isolette. Despite Barry's having tried to prepare me, a current of shock jolted through me as I stared at the fragile little figure before me. Her head was smaller than my cupped hand.

When the baby's breathing monitor sounded, the attending nurse quickly reached in through a sleeve opening in the isolette to revive her. The woman was so calm! And then she asked the unthinkable. "Would you like to hold her?"

I was frozen. But Barry nodded, and the nurse got a blanket out of something that looked like a big bun-warmer and wrapped the baby up, tubes and all. Barry reached out and nestled her close. After a few moments he turned and extended the bundle to me.

I took it. The blanket seemed to wrap around something that wasn't there. Yet the instant I cradled her in my arms I felt a vibrancy, a magnetism that made me draw it close to my breast, my heart. *Kara.* Peeping between the folds, I saw her exquisitely sculpted face, a baby in miniature. I held her close within the circle of my arms, and the essence of my baby seemed to soak into my skin, making my very blood warmer.

Holding Kara, this baby God had created just for me, I felt a holy bond between us. The fear that tormented me before had gone.

I'd been afraid to love Kara for fear of losing her. But God had shown me that His love can't be limited by conditions or problems. Kara was His gift to me, and I knew in this instant that God would only give me something good. Whatever lay ahead, Kara was my child and God's child, and He would care for us both.

"I'd better put her back now," the nurse said. "But you can put your hand through the sleeve to touch her."

I pressed my lips to Kara's tiny face and handed her to the nurse.

EDITOR'S NOTE: After spending three months in the ICU nursery, Kara came home with Sandy and Barry, weighing four pounds six ounces. When this story was written, in 1983, she was a beautiful, healthy five-year-old.

My Lost Love
Jane Kemp Baker

AFTER THE CHRISTMAS DECORATIONS were put away, I began to think about the best spot for a gift I'd received from a dear friend—a wall-hanging with macrame knots woven around the letters L O V E.

But I couldn't find the hanging! Last time I'd looked, it had been under the Christmas tree. I asked my husband if he'd seen it. Absorbed in his newspaper, he mumbled, "Oh, I probably put it away with the Christmas ornaments. I'll look for it later." He went on reading and forgot about it.

The next day, resentfully, I went down to the basement and pulled out the boxes of ornaments myself. As I opened one after another without success, I grew more frustrated and angry. How careless my husband was! And he'd treated the problem so casually! All this waste of time was *his* fault.

Then, in the midst of my accusations, the irony of the situation struck me. I was searching for "Love" with a completely unloving spirit. "Lord," I said aloud, "there's no use my looking anymore. Please help me get my priorities straight."

On a Saturday morning, as my husband and I were having a quiet talk, I confessed how angry I had been with him. Now *he* began to look for the lost hanging — without success.

Then I had an idea. "Did you look in the artificial Christmas tree box?"

"No, but it wouldn't be there."

"Let's look," I urged.

There it was, right on top! We hugged. "I think the Lord wanted us to find it together," my husband said.

Whenever I look at my lost and found "Love" hanging, it reminds
me of a great truth: You can't find love
until you're *able* to love.
And how wonderful
to find love with
someone
else.

A Child's Wisdom

Lorna Beall

ONE DAY when I was teaching a Sunday school class of mentally retarded children, I handed out pictures of Jesus which had a rock placed near Him. Then I handed out separate pictures of a tiny boy in a sitting position, thinking that the children could paste him on the rock.

But one little girl promptly pasted him in Jesus' clasped arms.

I often think of the love and trust in this special child's

heart that made her see so clearly what many of

us never see — that we should always

place ourselves in His

loving arms.

He is our

rock.

PART 2

Simple Gestures

Hugs, pats, backrubs, holding hands—such small gestures convey a world of love, put hope and cheer back in our lives, and provide the comfort we need in times of suffering and pain. Old or young, success or failure, we still need to feel the touch of love, And if we're feeling unloved, perhaps we need to be on the lookout for the signs of love from those who aren't able to put their love into words—a kindly deed, a friendly phone call, the silent presence of a neighbor in our grief.

HUGS

Say It with a Hug
Marjorie Willsie

I RECENTLY CALLED on a new neighbor and allotted myself ten minutes for the call. *Just long enough,* I thought, *to invite her children to the community party and make her feel welcome.*

Something she said, though, revealed a common interest and we were off. Two hours had passed when I finally decided that I really must leave. Instead of shaking hands at the door, she impulsively threw her arms about me and gave me a big hug. "Oh," she laughed, "I'm so glad you stopped. You have no idea how lonely I've been!"

Until that moment I had not realized how lonely *I* was. I have a fine family and wonderful neighbors. Why should I feel lonely?

Thinking about it on the way home, I realized that none of my many friends had ever made such a spontaneous show of affection toward me. I knew they liked me, maybe even loved me, and I was certain of their loyalty to me; but none had ever hugged me.

I felt a bond with Joyce, whom I had just met, that was stronger than the friendship I felt for my other friends, and it was wonderful to feel appreciated!

The whole episode kept running through my mind. It started me thinking about the very special times in my life when people had reached out to me and given me strength, courage or comfort by just a touch. I wondered why we are so reluctant to show emotion. Why not bestow a hug, a pat on the back, or a sympathetic touch without fear of seeming silly?

There was the time years ago when our second child announced he was on his way. The room was cold and the night seemed unbearably long. The doctor had come and gone, remarking as he left that it was probably a false alarm. I watched my mother-in-law as she moved about the room stuffing rags in the cracks around the window, filling the old wood stove, keeping busy. I was not particularly close to her and, as I huddled by the fire, I felt all alone in my own miserable little world.

I closed my eyes and a tear rolled down my cheek, followed by many others. I let them roll.

Then something exceptional happened. My mother-in-law stopped, laid her arm across my shoulder and, without a word, hugged me briefly to her. As she resumed her chores I knew of a certainty that I was not alone anymore. That hug told me that there was someone who knew how I felt and who cared. A couple of hours later, with our new son snuggled beside me, I fell asleep still feeling the warmth of that hug.

Mothers are always hugging their little ones, and the children hug back, don't they? But what about the kids who are taller than their mothers? Hugging one's mother is square or something; and she doesn't hug *them* because she is afraid of offending them.

There was the time my eighteen-year-old son was leaving for work in Massachusetts. I drove him to a friend's house where he was to get his ride. I felt like he was going to another world. With moist eyes I watched them load his things into his friend's car; then suddenly everyone went into the house and left me standing there.

He had not said good-bye.

I waited until the tears began to spill down my cheeks too fast for me to wipe them away. I wasn't going to leave without saying good-bye and I wasn't going to run in and embarrass him.

Suddenly he came running down the path. He drew me close to him and said, "Mom, don't cry. I'll be careful and I'll be okay. I'll even write to you. Good-bye, Mom. Take care." The feel of that hug still lingers, warm and firm, around my shoulders.

Another time, I lay in a hospital bed next to a woman named Norma who was racked with pain. For several days, while we shared the room, we talked, sometimes in the middle of the night while she waited for the shot to give her an hour or two of rest. She knew she was going to have to have more operations and much more pain. But after that there would be a chance to get more schooling, to learn a profession, and time to spend with her adopted son.

When I was ready to be discharged, I suddenly found myself with nothing to say. Simple words of cheer rang hollow, and prayer seemed oddly out of place just then. We had prayed together during the night.

So I did the only thing that seemed right. Leaning down, I touched each shoulder as gently as I could and kissed her cheek. I knew that even a tender touch hurt her; but there was a bond of love and understanding there, and with it the faith that someday she would make her dreams come true.

There are times when money and gifts won't help and kind words
sound flat and meaningless. Such a time may be the
occasion when a hug or a touch of affection
will be all you have to give. If so, give it
unreservedly and feel the
blessing go two
ways.

The Touching Gesture
Carol Kuykendall

I'LL NEVER FORGET the touching gesture of a friend late one evening several years ago. Unexpectedly, we found ourselves in the hospital with a very sick child and a grim diagnosis: juvenile diabetes. It was the end of an emotionally exhausting day. Lynn had gone home to be with our two daughters, and I was sitting by Derek's bed in the darkened room, watching the IV solution slowly drip down the tube into his arm. Even though I closed my eyes, the bubbling sound was an eerie reminder of where I was.

I heard a gentle knock on the door and looked up. There stood my friend, a mother who taught Sunday school with me.

"I just wanted to hug you," she said simply, and with those words and that gesture, she helped soothe my hurt. She also communicated the meaning of friendship. She was there. She cared. She understood.

Many times since then, I've hesitated to reached out to a friend in need, afraid my words would sound shallow or inappropriate.

But then I remember the image of my friend, standing there in the hospital doorway. I hear her words again—"I just wanted to hug you." And I reach out to others, knowing that the gesture is more important than the words.

The Comforter

Elaine St. Johns

MY DAUGHTER'S CALL from the hospital emergency room reached me at the convalescent home where I was visiting my ninety-three-year-old mother. My granddaughter Robin, just turned six, had fallen from the high bar at school, injuring her mouth severely. I picked up her sisters, aged two and four, and spent a hectic, tense afternoon supervising the little ones while awaiting Kris's return with Robin.

The doctor had taken eight stitches inside her mouth, six on the outside, and, as the little ones swarmed over their mother, Robin sat squarely in the biggest chair in the living room. Her face puffed almost beyond recognition, her long hair still ropey with dried blood, she looked tiny and forlorn. Still, I approached her cautiously, for Robin is the least demonstrative, the most private of children.

"Is there anything you want, darling?" I asked.

She looked me squarely in the eye and said, "I want a hug."

Me, too! I thought, as I cuddled her on my lap. *But how and whom does an exhausted grandmother ask?* As we rocked gently the words came: "I will pray the Father, and he shall give you another Comforter, that he may abide with you for ever" (John 14:16).

So I asked, just as simply as Robin had done—and just as simply felt the everlasting arms enfold us.

Sharing My Heart
Sue Monk Kidd

S OME TIME AGO my husband and I spent a weekend as volunteers in a shelter for the homeless in Atlanta. I'd read an article that said the homeless were America's invisible people. *Well, that certainly isn't true here,* I thought, as we arrived at the shelter door. I could see plenty of them.

While men wandered in from the streets, I busied myself in the kitchen. I inspected the pantry, stirred and re-stirred the stew, cleaned the sink. The men seemed to keep their distance. I didn't talk to one all evening.

But the next night after dinner, an old man came and stood at the kitchen door. His gray hair was blown in wild tangles around his ears. I seemed to recognize his face vaguely from when I'd handed out plates of food. "My name is Al," he said. "I sure wish you would give me a hug."

I stared at him, wishing I had a pot to stir, a plate to fill. Anything but this. Some of the men had mental problems and strange requests were not so unusual. Still I hoped I hadn't heard right. "Did you say hug?" I asked weakly.

He nodded, a look of pleading in his watery old eyes. "My daughter used to hug me a long time ago," he said.

Suddenly I saw beyond the wild hair and dirty coat right into his heart. I knew it was not the men who'd kept their distance, but *I*. Even in the middle of a shelter, the homeless had been invisible to me. And I understood, perhaps better than ever before, that love was not only doing something *for* somebody, it was touching their lives with my own. It was crying with them, laughing with them, accepting them as individuals and sharing my own heart.

I looked at Al. Then I wrapped my arms around him and hugged him tight.

The Kindly Touch

So little means so very much,
An understanding glance and such;
A letter from a friend afar,
A baby's smile, a cookie jar.
So little means so very much,
Dear Lord, give me the kindly touch!

—Tom Hickey

PATS, BACKRUBS AND HOLDING HANDS

The Pat on the Back
Rick Hamlin

ON WEDNESDAY NIGHTS when I come home from work I go
directly to church where I help with the youth group — Chris,
Jenny, Judy, Paul, Chance, Claire, Shawn, Sandra. We get anywhere
from six to twenty junior high school kids at our weekly meetings.
Together we sing songs, put on plays, do skits, play charades, study the
Bible, delve into our problems and, most important, pray.

Sometimes, though, I'm too tired to attend these meetings and wish
I were going home instead; but once I'm there, the kids always pick me
up. Such as the other night when I was pouring juice during our
refreshment hour. Suddenly I felt a tentative tap on my shoulder. I
turned around to see Chris — our break-dancing champ — beside me.
"Yes?" I asked. "Did you want something?"

"Nothing," he said shyly, shrugging his shoulders. "That was just a
pat on the back." Then he paused, "We all need one every once in a
while."

That's what my Wednesday night friends give me, a thousand pats
on the back. In more formal language it's called Christian fellowship,
but I like Chris's way of seeing it.

Once in a while, when it's least expected, it's nice to *show* our care,
one for another.

What You Need
Doris Haase

İT WAS THE DAY AFTER CHRISTMAS. I hadn't been feeling well and went to see my doctor. Three hours later I found myself in the hospital. I have always disliked hospitals and the next five days were frightening. How I longed for home!

Then, on the fourth day when my spirits were lowest, a new morning nurse came into my room. Her smile was bright.

"What you need," she announced cheerfully, "is a good rubdown!"

In a matter of moments her strong, gentle fingers were massaging me with a sweet-smelling lotion while my body, and mood, relaxed. Tingling and grateful, I thanked her as she left to complete her rounds. Home at last, I found a friend had cleaned my apartment. A beautiful flower arrangement greeted me from the dining room table. My refrigerator had been filled. And my cup overflowed.

Never before had I more fully realized how much
expressions of love can cheer a heavy heart. And
never again do I want to forget. In fact, I have
resolved to pass this love along every
chance I get — by considering
what someone may need,
and whether I
can give it.

Touch of Hands
Linda Ching Sledge

MY FATHER doesn't talk much. My mother and I, however, spill over with words. We are never at a loss to describe our feelings, to tell stories, to offer advice. I often felt sorry for my father for not having the natural eloquence that we women did.

My last visit home to Hawaii, my birthplace, showed me how wrong about him I was. I was sitting talking with my mother in my grandfather's living room one afternoon. From where we sat, I could see into the bedroom where my grandfather, who is ninety-five, spends his days.

My eyes fell on my father, who was rubbing lotion onto my grandfather's arms. My grandfather lay on the bed, looking up at his eldest son. I had seen my father do this scores of times, but this time I saw the care with which he touched his father's gnarled fingers. I marveled at the tenderness with which he laid his hands on the age-spotted shoulders. Finally, I noticed the light shining in the old man's face as he drew strength from his son's fierce, protective love.

My father inarticulate? Not at all. Neither my mother nor I could convey so well in words what my father did through the touch of his hands.

Holding Hands
Elaine St. Johns

Someone very dear to me has been in a convalescent home for many months now. When I first began visiting her, I was shy, awkward, unsure how best to express what I felt. So I had great sympathy for an eager group of high school students who had formed an Adopt-a-Grandparent club and were standing around nervously eyeing their wheelchair clients, reluctant to "begin."

"What do we *do?*" one youth asked me. "What do they like to think *about?*"

"I think what they like best," I said, "is holding hands. If you just sit beside them and hold hands, you can talk about anything—or nothing."

I told him of the day I discovered this when I found a large semicircle of wheelchair residents gathered in quiet joy around a young priest. He had finished his talk and was going from one to the other, holding hands with each as he bid them good-bye. My own particular lady put her cheek against his hands and I saw tears fall.

"What did he say to you?" I had asked.

"He told us each one of us was special to God," she said.

There were those in the group who couldn't take in the words. I had always been a little embarrassed by the cult of "touching," even feeling superior to such sentimental shenanigans. Now I saw that what they all understood was God's love coming to them through the concerned touch of a fellow man.

I have since found this a universal language—with children as well as the aged, with strangers as well as friends. The authentic handshake, the encouraging pat on the back, the spontaneous hug, holding hands—all can say what words cannot: "You are special to God—and to me."

SILENT SIGNS

Unspoken Words
Dick Enberg

I ALWAYS LOVED and admired my father. He was a good provider, working hard for us during the week in a Detroit factory and the rest of the time on our forty-acre fruit farm. But good and solid as he was, for me he had one shortcoming: He was not a demonstrative man.

I can remember how frustrating that was when I was a kid. In our small Michigan town, I was a starting player on the high school varsity football, basketball and baseball teams, but rarely did he congratulate me on a victory or a good game. Even when I scored twenty-two points in one basketball game, all Dad said was, "How many points did the man you covered score?"

Years later, when I was living alone in California, leading the harried life of a TV sportscaster, Dad, who had been living alone on the farm back in Michigan, came to live with me. He planted fruit trees in my backyard and cared for them like the cherry, apple and plum trees back home. He could fix anything, and I'd tell him what a master carpenter he was. But still there was little praise about me and my work.

Then came his long, fatal struggle with cancer. Throughout those difficult months, I longed for an open hug from him whenever I told him I loved him, or at least a quiet, unsolicited "I love you, Son." But even on his deathbed Dad was as taciturn as always.

Later, however, I began to think about Dad and me. Maybe he had been quick to criticize and slow to compliment me, but he'd been there—for every game. And then one day, cleaning out his bedroom, I came across a half-dozen shoe boxes. Inside were hundreds of audio-tapes, carefully labeled, filed and stored. They were marked with things like "Louisville vs. UCLA Basketball, 1978," "Rams vs. Cowboys, 1973." They were tapes of the games I had broadcast, tapes Dad had secretly made by placing the microphone of his small recorder next to the radio or television speaker.

We know how important it is to hear our loved ones tell us that we are loved. But shouldn't we also be aware of the *unspoken* words of love? Those tapes told me how much my father cared. And I thought of our Heavenly Father, whom we never see or touch, but the evidence of whose caring is everywhere. All those years with Dad, I just needed to look for the signs of love.

Small Signs
Aletha Jane Lindstrom

I'D BEEN FEELING UNLOVED LATELY. Nothing serious—just no hugs, no kisses, no "I love you's." Then I recalled the words of Elizabeth Barrett Browning: "How do I love thee? Let me count the ways." This reminded me that some folks (myself included) have difficulty putting love into words. So I decided one day to "count the ways." I made the following list. It's not earth-shattering I know, but these simple overlooked acts made me feel loved again:

1. *My husband Carl's* handing me his sweater as I headed for the mailbox. "Better put this on. The wind's mighty chilly."
2. *Our son Tim's* calling from Virginia to ask, "Everything okay?"
3. *Our daughter-in-law Jessica's* note: "Wish you were here. The yard's filled with bluebirds!"
4. *My friend Gayla's* phone call: "Missed you at the meeting yesterday. I didn't enjoy it without you."
5. *My faithful collie's* loving look as she rested her head gently on my knee.
6. *And,* above all, *God's* encompassing, unfailing love.

Are there small signs of love around that you've taken for granted? Count them now and
thank your lucky
stars.

A Love Loaf
Mary Jane Meyer

SEVERAL YEARS AGO, the women's group in our church gave each member a small, plastic bank fashioned after a freshly baked loaf of bread. It was called a "love loaf." I put the love loaf in an easily accessible place in the kitchen and, in addition to our adult children who happened by, I noticed my husband dropping in his pocket change on several occasions. The love loaf filled with amazing speed and was returned to the church to fulfill its intended purpose of helping to feed the hungry of the world. It was easy. It was self-satisfying, and it was fun.

In fact, I was so taken with the idea of the love loaf that I have set up a "family" love loaf of my own. Now, when one of our family members or a close friend needs cheering up, I dip into my love loaf so I can take them some small, inexpensive gift: a bag of their favorite hard candies, a new coloring book for a little one, a bright hair ribbon, maybe some ripe, luscious fruit.

Why don't you start your love loaf today? Any container will do.
And you may even want to drop some "promissory notes"
along with the coins: an evening of baby-sitting,
your special tuna casserole or an hour
of reading and letter-writing.
What an easy way to
love one another.

I Wonder

What would happen if each drop
Of rain refused to fall,
Or every sunbeam ceased to shine
Because it was so small?

What would happen if each day
We chose to leave undone
An act of kindness just because
It was a little one?

— Esther F. Thom

Being There
Madge Harrah

WHEN I WAS FIFTEEN years old, my parents took me with them late one afternoon to visit an elderly neighbor who lay dying. For an hour we sat with her in a deep twilight silence, although occasionally she and my mother and father exchanged gentle smiles. I squirmed uncomfortably in my chair, wondering why no one spoke.

Several years after that I lost a beloved brother, and I was utterly inconsolable. There was absolutely nothing anyone could say to me that eased my heartache. Then one afternoon an old and dear friend came to my home, gave me a warm hug and sat down with me, saying nothing. Her very presence was a comfort far beyond the power of any words she might have spoken.

So today I would like to share with you something I've finally learned. It's simply this: Don't ever be afraid to go to someone who is contending with an extreme problem or a deep sorrow even though you think you don't know what to say. Just *be there*. That's all. For sometimes God's healing love can best embrace and comfort us when we are still, silent, joined as one in communion with Him.

PART 3

Unexpected Actions

Because love is focused on the other person, it always does the right thing — which may be wonderfully creative, like a child helping his blind mother to "see" the expression on his school picture, or a wife finding a way to get a forgotten lunch to her husband. Or, it may seem absolutely wrong — like holding out a hand to a menacing wildcat. And sometimes it may look quite crazy — like a guard helping an angry and abusive prisoner learn to write out his abuse, or a couple deciding to adopt five boys at once. Love finds the creative way to meet the need, to challenge indifference, anger and hatred. And in every case the unexpected action that may even have looked silly or ridiculous or wrong was exactly the right one.

They Took Us All!
*Mildred Jones**
as told to Etta Lynch

BEN AND I HAD BEEN MARRIED ten years and had prayed earnestly for children nine of these years. Both of us had enjoyed many brothers and sisters as we grew up and the thought of a childless marriage struck terror in our hearts. Finally, because there seemed to be no alternative, we tackled the endless red tape that accompanies adoption of children. We decided to adopt one, then wait two years to adopt a second child.

Within two months the agency director called us. "Could you and your husband come down to the office? We'd like to talk to you."

I was almost stammering with excitement. "Is it a boy or a girl?"

"Well, we'd like to discuss a few things with you before we say much." It occurred to me that he was hedging, and I was puzzled.

We made an appointment for that afternoon after Ben came in from work, and the director plunged immediately into the most incredible story. "We have brothers that are adoptable, but they're not infants. Let me tell you a little about their background."

There followed an account of an unbelievably tragic life their mother had led: having too many children too close together, illness, marriage to an irresponsible man, often in trouble and finally being

---

*All names have been changed

abandoned by him. There came a time when she had no choice, and she gave the children out for adoption.

Tears stood in my eyes, and without hesitation I cried, "We'll take them both!"

The director looked discomfited and cleared his throat. "Well, Mrs. Jones, there aren't just two."

"But how many then?"

Without answering, he rose abruptly and asked us to come with him. Opening the door to a large playroom, he indicated a group of boys at the farthest end. The oldest boy in the group looked us over appraisingly and went back to his checker game. "Your move, Larry." He prodded his partner. The younger faces remained turned toward us. The oldest boy said loudly, "Get smart. Ain't nobody gonna take all five of us. We seen 'em come in before, and they all wanta split us up. Fergit it, and play!"

The four smaller faces continued their silent entreaty, and the combined battery of their beseeching eyes broke my heart. I was flabbergasted, and when I looked at Ben, his mouth was helplessly agape. I stammered, "You mean, all five are brothers?" The director nodded. "And you mean . . ." He shut the door so the boys couldn't hear.

"Yes, I mean they're all brothers, and they all need parents. We've tried placing them singly, but they're so miserable it hasn't worked at all. You're our last hope. Do you think you could possibly see your way clear to adopting five boys?" He smiled wryly, as though he knew what he asked was impossible.

My mind whirled. This was fantastic! We were financially able, but five boys . . . ! Then I thought suddenly of our agreement that we wouldn't ever rear a child alone if we had a choice. We'd planned to wait perhaps two years and adopt a second child. Now, we had a choice. We had prayed for children, and here was our family, through the difficult bottle and diaper stage — and desperately in need of a mother and a father.

"Ben, I want to take them all, please?" I begged, anticipating protests that there'd be too much work and responsibility. I underestimated him, for he took all of thirty seconds to agree. The director was visibly moved. He asked us to wait outside while he told the boys.

When he opened the door of the playroom, I caught a glimpse of the smallest boy's face, and it was lit with wonder. Over and over he was repeating incredulously, "They took us all! Wow! They took us all!" Those words and the look on that little face have sustained us through the hard times.

Our boys were nine, eight, seven, six and five, and they all bore a strong family resemblance. When we took them from the orphanage in the new outfits we'd bought them, my heart almost burst with pride. My five sons! Each handsome with his special good feature: a ready smile, startlingly beautiful eyes, hair black as a moonless night. And even if they hadn't been good-looking boys, our love made them so.

When word leaked out that we'd done such a foolhardy thing as adopting five male children, our telephone rang continuously. A newspaper wanted to run a feature story. Art Linkletter called, wanting us to appear on his television program. Then Gary Moore called us to make our adoption of five our "secret" on his program "I've Got a Secret." Ben and I are both retiring by nature, and we quaked at the thought of publicity. We have refused all offers and still feel that notoriety wouldn't serve any useful purpose. All we'd wanted was a child, and circumstances had given us five.

I laughingly tell my friends that my problem was childlessness, and I exchanged it for chaos, but there isn't a single regret. There have been crises without number. Ben and I have made mistakes. But when my boys are sitting side by side in church, playing baseball together, or crowded around the table at mealtime, I know then that there's one mistake we didn't make — that of wrenching these brothers apart when they enjoy such closeness.

Occasionally I still run across a bit of scrap of paper that contains last night's homework, mysterious doodlings, and somewhere over in a corner, retraced again and again for emphasis, those four words that make me realize these boys never have taken their good fortune for granted . . . THEY TOOK US ALL.

Love Understands
Pat Embrey

I T WAS THE DAY the children brought their class photos home from school for their parents to see.

They wanted me, their mother, to express an opinion, but I couldn't because I am blind. I felt so inadequate. The best I could do was cheerfully assure them that their grandmothers would be happy to receive any picture of them.

But that wasn't good enough. They stood in front of me uncertainly for a moment. Then quite unexpectedly my six-year-old son, Chris, solved the problem. He said, "Mama, I smiled; but my picture isn't smiling! It looks like this." And he put my fingertips on his lips and showed me a solemn expression.

Then Missy, my five-year-old daughter, followed his example and showed me her expression. I was overwhelmed. I had not known that such a large amount of understanding could come from the tiny hearts of children. And while they happily put the pictures in envelopes to send to their grandmothers, I thanked God for the joy of knowing such love.

Warm Cookies
Cathy Burden Griebner

Two years ago my daughter experienced the loss of a good friend, an elderly lady down the street whom she had adopted as her extra grandmother and was in the habit of stopping in to visit. She took the news of the sudden death first with tears, and then with protests of bitterness. Finally, she became maternal and began to worry about the elderly husband who was left alone. One day she decided to bake him some cookies, which had to be delivered while they were still warm.

"Because, Mom," she explained, "anybody can buy homemade cookies, but only a wife can bring them warm from the oven for the first taste."

Somehow I felt that my daughter possessed a wisdom far beyond her years in that simple explanation. And for me, the meaning of real thoughtfulness will always be remembered in those two words, "warm cookies."

A Creative Solution
James McDermott

RECENTLY AS I LISTENED to the nightly news, it seemed as if all I heard were problems ranging from small to large, and no one seemed to be doing anything about them. *Doesn't anyone care enough to find a way to change things?* I asked myself. *Surely there are creative people in the world who care about others.*

The next day, I called my absent-minded friend Ansel Tuthill to borrow a tool. When I went to get it, he told me a story that restored my faith in the creativity and caring of people.

Ansel had left on a day-long sailing adventure last summer, when — about an hour after he'd departed — his wife, Jean, discovered on a kitchen counter the sack lunch she'd made for him. She knew that he would have cast off from the dock by this time and that probably it would be impossible to intercept him. But she didn't give up.

"Maybe I can catch him at the bridge," she thought out loud, "before he gets out into open water." So she jumped in her car and sped off to a bridge she knew Ansel would have to pass under. Ten minutes later, she'd parked the car and run out on the bridge walkway . . . just in time to drop the lunch in his outstretched arms. Ansel gave her a wave and a grateful smile.

Are the odds stacked against you in a problem that you are facing today? Don't give up. If you care enough, maybe you'll be inspired by an unusual solution!

Jubilee!
*Judy Hart**

"P LE-E-E-EZ, LET'S TALK," I begged for the umpteenth time.
"Get out of my sight," he snapped, and stormed out of the
kitchen.

The now-familiar lump tightened in my throat. Teary-eyed, I
dropped into a kitchen chair, crying, "Lord, what's happening to us?"
How proud I'd been when Dan quit drinking! How perfect life was
going to be. Now I laughed at my simple-minded optimism, my great
expectations. Alcohol had been Dan's best friend; when he was forced
to quit drinking he'd sunk into a stony, severe depression. For six
months he'd refused to speak, stalking past me as if I were invisible; at
most, he'd snarl "Get lost" or "Go away." After twenty-one years of
marriage, we were headed for divorce.

That night, I buried my head under the covers, pleading, "O Lord,
help me!" I wanted to sleep forever.

Morning found me worn and weary. Before, I'd always prayed for
wisdom, insight and healing, but this morning I cried out in full
helplessness: "Lord, please show me what to *do* — I don't want this
marriage to end!"

As I went through my Bible, Leviticus 25:10 seemed to leap from

---

*Names have been changed.

the page: "And ye shall hallow the fiftieth year, and proclaim liberty throughout all the land unto all the inhabitants thereof: it shall be a jubilee unto you . . ."

That scripture haunted me all day. Dan's fiftieth birthday was only three weeks away. Was the Lord telling me I should honor his fiftieth year? And if so, in what way? Maybe a birthday party. No, that would be ridiculous. How could I throw Dan a party? We weren't even speaking.

A week passed and that Bible verse still sat in my mind. Even the crazy idea of a party. Finally I thought, *Okay, I'll invite our friends Jane and George for a cookout the Sunday before Dan's birthday. After all, fifty years of life is special.*

I called, half-hoping they couldn't make it, but Jane accepted. "It's a surprise," I said just before hanging up. I couldn't believe I'd done it.

Four days before the cookout, Dan and I sat on the patio, each pretending to be alone. After weeks of near-total silence, a tense conversation started. Before long it had blazed into an argument. Through gritted teeth Dan snarled, "This isn't working anymore; I want out," and he left.

"Get out, then," I hissed at his departing back. Alone with my whirling thoughts, I cried: "Lord, how wrong I was! You didn't want a jubilee; I just imagined it. I'm sorry, but I hate him." What a foolish idea, planning a party under circumstances like these. It was like arranging deck chairs on the *Titanic. I'm calling Jane to cancel,* I thought. *I want out too.*

Just then Dan came back. He must have felt bad, for he said in a surprisingly casual tone, "We have such nice neighbors. It's too bad they haven't been over more often."

Suddenly, my depression lifted and my spirit soared as a voice sounded inside: *Jubilee—a celebration!*

I held my breath. I wanted to laugh, or shout. Instead, I jumped out of my lawn chair and into the house to make phone calls—not to cancel the cookout, but to invite all our other neighbors and friends! Amazingly, all the people I called said they'd be delighted to came and offered to bring something. I happily accepted.

Next afternoon, as I stood contemplating an unmade bed, I overheard Dan on the phone with our family doctor. He'd badly pulled a muscle in his back. The prescription was hot, half-hour-long baths, four times a day. What a fix! Now I had thirty-two people coming for a surprise party, and I had a dirty house and a bed-ridden husband who "wanted out"—yet somehow I knew everything would be fine. I can't explain how, but I *knew* that this party was the right thing to do. Was I crazy, doing all this for a man who wouldn't speak to me? No . . . for the first time in my life I felt mysteriously, truly inspired.

That night, I slept like a baby, certain I was doing what God wanted me to do.

Saturday, the day before the party, I wanted to make Dan's favorite potato salad. I boiled a party-size pot of potatoes without his noticing. But where would I cool them? I put them in a grocery bag and hid them in the trash. A stroke of genius! When Dan took his next therapeutic bath, I retrieved my potatoes, made the world's fastest potato salad, and hid it safely, way in the back of the refrigerator.

A little later our former neighbors the Bakers phoned. They'd be in town for a three-day convention—could their daughter, Nancy (our fifteen-year-old daughter Trish's friend), bunk in with us? The last thing I needed was an overnight guest, but on second thought it gave me the perfect excuse for some frantic housecleaning. Trish, who was in on my plans, whirled into action, scrubbing and dusting and vacuuming and polishing.

By this time I was in a trance. Floating out the door toward the supermarket, I saw a party-supply store. Decorations! I'd almost forgotten! I bought balloons, crepe-paper streamers, a HAPPY 50TH BIRTHDAY banner, matching plates and napkins, and lots of candles. While Dan soaked, I hid in the guest room and inflated twenty-five balloons. It was a blessing he was ignoring me, or he might have wondered why my face was blue. All day long Trish sneaked to and from my neighbor Jane's, carrying ground meat, cheese, pickles, hamburger buns, ice cream. "Take this to Jane's," I barked like a drill sergeant. "Buy this! Borrow that from Jane."

Sunday! Party day was here! Everything was all set, except how to get Dan out of the house. The guests were coming at six. During church I prayed for a solution. As we were leaving, Trish's boyfriend, Eric, asked if I needed help. I told him about getting Dan away from home.

"I'll take care of it," Eric said. Who'd have guessed Eric would be the answer to a prayer?

At 5:20 P.M. the Bakers arrived, depositing Nancy and her luggage. Still no word from Eric. What did he have planned?

By 5:30 my stomach was churning at high speed. At 5:35 the phone rang and I jumped, spilling my iced tea.

"Hi, Lynne, is Dan there? It's Jim." Eric's father! So that's who Eric had enlisted!

"Dan, telephone!" I called, with a silent thank you. Dan fell for Jim's crazy story — that he needed a lift home — and made a quick exit.

When he left, I resumed my sergeant's role: "Hang the balloons and crepe streamers! Hang the birthday banner! Bring all the chairs from the basement!" Jane hurried in through the kitchen with the food.

At six o'clock sharp, in came the guests, carrying beautiful salads, pies, cakes. Instantly, my picnic table was a marvelous crammed display suitable for the cover of *Better Homes and Gardens*. And Trish had baked a big lovely birthday cake at Jane's. With its few errors camouflaged by fifty strategically placed candles, the cake had a warmth and charm that only youth could create. It was the perfect centerpiece.

"We're ready," I breathed — just as our sentry shouted, "He's here!" Everyone hurried to the front door, and as Dan entered, we shouted, "SURPRISE!" He gazed in astonishment at the people and at the brightly decorated rooms, and staggered backward against the door.

"You got me!" he exclaimed. "You really got me!"

Dan stood leaning against the door, totally shocked. Running to him, Trish gave him a big kiss, saying, "Happy birthday, Daddy!"

I followed, kissing him and squeaking, through the catch in my throat, "Happy birthday, dear."

After eating, and before opening his presents, Dan asked for our attention. He thanked God for Trish and me, for helping us stick together through the tough times, and for such wonderful friends. My heart leapt as his eyes sought mine while he spoke. Tears of joy, not pain, welled up inside me. He said this party was the most wonderful thing that had ever happened to him.

My tears finally flowed when Dan wrapped me in his arms and kissed me, the first kiss in a long, long time. "This is fantastic. I can't thank you enough, Lynne," he whispered in my ear. His warm, muscular body felt so comfortable and right as I hugged him. I wanted to hold on forever.

A friend provided a big Roman candle, which we lit at dusk. The spectacular, dancing gold jets, shooting up into the night sky to our oohs and ahhs, made the perfect ending to a jubilant day.

From that night on, Dan and I were on the road back. Sure, we needed help, mostly from a chemical-dependency counselor who helped us as Dan and I both strove for understanding on our often-difficult path to recovery. But the worst was over. We'd won.

One evening a year after Dan's jubilee party, I heard Dan say to our minister, "You know, there was a time when I was deeply depressed and God showed me love in an overwhelming way. That was a watershed moment for me." As we drove home, I asked Dan what he'd meant.

He looked at me, his eyebrows lifted in astonishment, and said,
"Why, the birthday party, of course. It showed me what
I'd been too blind to see — that you still loved me,
and what we had was worth saving.
Lynne, that birthday party
saved our marriage, and
maybe it saved
my life."

Outwitted

He drew a circle that shut me out —
Heretic, rebel, a thing to flout.
But Love and I had the wit to win:
We drew a circle that took him in.

— Edwin Markham

The Lady and the Wildcat
Enid Melrose

WHEN I RECENTLY RETIRED at age eighty-three from nursing in New York City, I retreated alone to my cottage in New England. It stands at the foot of a mountain, part of the White Mountain Range.

This is isolated country, sparsely settled. Wild animals abound in such terrain and the valley back of my mountain is noted for an abundance of wildcats.

One warm afternoon last fall, when the autumn leaves were exceptionally brilliant, I couldn't resist the temptation to bask in the sun for a while by the front stone steps. Armed with two large pillows and a magazine, I started outdoors. The front door was swollen shut from recent rains, and I was unable to open it. I went out by the shed door and walked around a clump of shrubbery to reach the front door. I stretched out on my pillows by the steps, which face a long lane leading from the end of the cottage.

It was about 4:00, a restful hour in these mountains. After reading about twenty minutes, a feeling of great danger suddenly came over me.

I quickly looked up and stared straight into the face of a full-grown wildcat, only about twelve feet from me.

He stood with one foot advanced, crouched as though to spring, staring directly into my eyes. I was too frightened to move. His face looked perfectly round, about the size of a large plate, and was covered with bristling gray hair with white on each side, extending from his ears around the sides of his face to his chin. He had large, gold-colored eyes, in the centers of which were piercing black pupils. There we were, staring at each other, neither of us seeming even to breathe!

The first thought that came to my mind was that I would have a better chance standing up than lying down, so I slowly rose to my feet, alert to the possibility that he might attack me. He kept staring, not even moving a muscle. With a shock I recalled that the front door, directly back of me, was stuck. If I ran for the back door, I would have to go directly toward the wildcat to get around the shrubbery. I didn't dare try this. If he thought I was attacking him, he would surely spring upon me in self-defense. I was cornered.

In past experiences in the woods, I have had intuitional warnings of imminent danger. I have learned to recognize them as God's inner spiritual protection. The Bible says that God sends His Holy Spirit (the power of God) as a Comforter and that He dwells within our spirit (John 14:26). I believe this, and I have often felt God's presence, especially when thinking about Him or breathing a quick prayer for help in an emergency.

Now, standing there afraid and completely motionless, I prayed, "God, I need You!" Immediately, all fear vanished, and in its place came a strange but great warm wave of love for that wildcat. I couldn't understand it but, without thinking, I leaned forward and held out my hand and called to him as I would to a pet kitten, "Kitty, kitty, kitty," extending to the cat my hand and that extraordinary feeling of love.

All this time he had been wildly staring at me, his threatening eyes glued to mine, never moving a muscle, remaining in that same crouched position, ready to spring at any moment. Nevertheless, I felt love so strongly that I wanted to touch the wildcat's head to pet him. Such an attitude was foreign to my normal instinct and knowledge of handling wild animals, but I knew it was from God in answer to my prayer for His help.

As I still gazed at the wildcat, he turned about and walked with long, quick strides down the lane; then he whirled around facing me again. I thought surely he had decided to come charging back—he looked so wild and threateningly at me—but God again sent that strong wave of love over me. I called to the cat as before, "Kitty, kitty, kitty, kitty," and extended that same hand of love out to him. He turned again down the lane. I repeated the call three times. And each time I felt a stronger love for the animal.

The last time he stopped was when he reached a brook that flows over the lane at the edge of the yard. There he took a stance on the culvert, then followed the brook into the woods.

I breathed a prayer of gratitude to God for this wonderful evidence of His abundant love for all His creatures. I have never doubted that it was God's love which was transmitted to me—the power of love which had somehow calmed the wildcat and protected me.

Then the thought came to me that perhaps I had seen a
demonstration of the way beast and bird and man
had, at the morning of creation, lived
together in harmony and peace, as
God originally
intended.

Message from an Angry Man

E. L. Allen

PRISON INMATES often commit crimes while in confinement, and when they do, they are arrested and sent to a jail within the jail. These areas are called adjustment centers and their purpose is to restore the culprit to the institution's main population as a useful, nonviolent citizen — which is sometimes a difficult task.

Some years ago I was custody sergeant in charge of a California prison adjustment center when an inmate who had attempted to kill a fellow prisoner was assigned there. I knew he was going to be a problem. He didn't want to be in my area and I let him know that I didn't like having him.

From the moment he was confined, he looked for ways of disrupting the program, other inmates and my staff. No one liked him and he had vowed to kill the first officer who opened his door. He spent hours and hours kicking his room door; he would yell and scream until I thought he would pass out from exhaustion — but no such luck.

Every morning as I passed his cell on my way to the office, he would suddenly leap from his bed, violently kick his door and shout obscenities at me.

This went on for several weeks. Finally I approached his cell one morning very quietly, opened the door and said, "You know, you're spending all this time and energy kicking your door, losing sleep and upsetting yourself when there is a much simpler way to insult me. Why don't you print what you want to call me on a poster and display it in your window before you go to bed at night? Then you won't have to go through the aggravation of getting up early and forcing yourself to remain awake wondering what time I'm going to arrive for duty."

He sat up in bed and for a long moment looked at me as if he couldn't believe what he had just heard. He rubbed his eyes and said, "You must be some kind of a nut."

We talked for a while and his portion of the conversation was bitter and abusive. Eventually he agreed that a sign would take a lot less effort but he then confided that he was unable to read or write.

"Tell you what let's do," I said. "I'll show you how to print the word you want to call me, and my name. You make several posters and when you're through, I'll select the best one. Then each morning when I come in, have it in your window. I'll be insulted and you can have some sleep."

For three days he labored diligently, spending all of his free time printing the signs. I then selected one that was particularly neat and praised him for the effort. Each morning for the next two weeks the sign was brightly displayed to greet my arrival.

On Monday of the third week I visited his room once again and asked if he would care to learn additional words that were not profane and that would help him learn to read. He said that he would.

I managed to get a few second-grade schoolbooks and with those, together with daily room visits and his own desire to learn, he eventually was able to write a letter to his parents.

During the time I studied with him he continued to be bitter and each day he displayed the obscene sign. I was beginning to wonder if my effort to help him was worth the trouble. Helping to create an obscene sign was not in keeping with my religious beliefs but I was trying desperately to break the shell he had built around himself. I felt I was failing.

After a weekend off-duty I found myself dreading the return to work and that foul sign — but return I must. As I approached this inmate's cell, I was surprised to find that the sign was not on display. I stood there for a moment, wondering why, and what he was up to, when suddenly he leaped from his bed and kicked the door in the same vengeful way he had done in the past. My first thought was, *Not again.* But my discouragement quickly faded when he smiled and held up a sign that read:

GOD BLESS YOU SARGENT —
GLAD YOUR BACK

PART 4

The Right Words

Love does need to be expressed in words. And the right words at the right time can provide exactly the pickup needed in times of discouragement or difficulty. "Let me help you," "You can do it," even a simple "Good work" or "Thank you" can express care and concern. The right words often come from children, whose simplicity, love and faith enables them to say the very thing needed to change a situation or meet a need. And in the difficult days when aging loved ones seem to lose their minds and their personalities, even there love can elicit the right words.

Mighty Little Note
Adrian DeGalan

WHEN I WAS A FIRST-YEAR TEACHER, Debbie was one of my favorite students. No one could resist her; she was cute as a button with her curly brown hair and big brown eyes. Deb had a way of melting your heart.

My second year was to be spent in a large class, squeezed into a tiny, old basement classroom. It was a bit discouraging to see all the desks crammed close together with little room to pass among the students.

A few days after the start of school I opened my desk to take attendance one morning. I found a small, white piece of paper in the desk drawer. On it was written: "I know forty *very* lucky kids!" It was signed Debbie.

I can't tell you how good it made me feel. I will always remember
that as the most pleasant beginning to a school year
that I have ever had. My sagging morale was
sent soaring by a kind note from
a loving eleven-year-old
girl.

Plant Flower Seeds
Aletha Jane Lindstrom

OUR WORDS CAN HAVE a tremendous impact on those whose lives touch ours. I thought seriously about this when I received a church bulletin recently. "When we speak words of love," it read, "we plant 'flower seeds.' Negative words beget 'weed seeds.' " Because I love flowers, this message appealed to me. I long to plant "flower seeds," but I often lack the proper words. The bulletin suggested using these "flower seed" phrases:

> *Good Work!*
> *Let me help you.*
> *I forgive you.*
> *Congratulations!*
> *I'm sorry.*
> *Thank you.*
> *I love you.*

I've copied this list on a card and glued a photo of one of my favorite flowers — a columbine — on the back. Each time I use one of these sentences, I put a check mark beside it. I hope this soon becomes a habit, producing flowers that seed and reseed in an endlessly widening garden.

Has your garden been overrun lately with weeds of anger or resentment, hurt or envy? Why not pluck them out and start planting "flower seeds" of hope, happiness, joy, contentment, peace. Water these "flower seeds" of yours and watch them grow tall.

"You Can Do It"
Samantha McGarrity

A LARGE WITHERING PLANT stood abandoned in our office. "Sam, why don't you take this one on?" a co-worker suggested, poking his head into my office. "Maybe you could save it."

"I don't know," I mumbled, looking around at the abundant pots of cheerful greenery that already surrounded me. I gave the plant an unsympathetic glance. It looked hopeless.

"Come on, Sam, he'd fit right into that sunny corner."

"Oh all right," I reluctantly agreed. We tied up its stem with an old brown tie, watered it, and dusted off its lackluster leaves. Then we named it! Leif.

The plant became a center of attention. People dropped by to give it words of encouragement. "Come on, Leif, you can do it!" "Good morning, Leif, have a good day!" In just two weeks, Leif completely revived and towered proudly over my desk. I was amazed — and elated.

"Would you look at this plant!" I called out to everyone that day. "What a transformation."

"Plants aren't too different from people," Ginger, one of the secretaries replied. "A little love, and they perk right up." We all nodded, glowing in our triumph.

Looking at Leif today, I am reminded of the importance of giving love — so very essential to *all* of life. And then I taped this message to one of the plant's gigantic leaves: "People need perking up, too."

"I Want to Help You"
Nancy Thies Marshall

I POSED AND WAITED for the music to begin. Out of the corner of my eye I could see the Chinese and American gymnasts on the sidelines. We were competing in a historic gymnastic meet between our two countries. The Chinese athletes had not competed internationally since the 1950s, and it was the first time they had visited the United States since the Cultural Revolution began.

As the top-ranked Olympian competing that night in 1973 at New York's Madison Square Garden, I'd set out to win the all-around with the highest overall score. But after embarrassing falls from the balance beam and uneven bars, I had no hope of a first-place finish. Nevertheless I was still optimistic as I took my stance on the mat to do my floor-exercise routine.

At least I can redeem my pride by doing well on this event, I thought. But as I waited, all I heard through the speakers was garbled noise. *The sound man must have put the wrong tape in the machine*, I thought. I moved off the mat, looking to my coach for an explanation.

She cued me again. I went back to the mat only to hear the same muffled sounds. A knot tightened in my stomach. *I already blew my other routines! Now this!* I wanted to crawl under the mat and hide. I dreaded the prospect of performing my floor routine with no music. That would be like eating dry toast — boring and flavorless.

A fiddling with the tape ensued, and then came the same awful sounds groaning and echoing through the Garden.

Muriel Grossfeld, my coach, hurried over. "You can perform without accompaniment . . . " *Oh, no,* I thought, shaking my head fiercely. "Or we can ask for help. The Chinese team has a pianist. We could ask him if he could improvise."

I shrugged and nodded. "Let's ask."

Muriel came back and whispered, "His name is Chou Chiasheng. He says he wants to help you."

What beautiful words to hear! Once again, I took my place on the mat. And the music began. Mr. Chou had never seen me practice, but his music matched my movements. We performed an unprecedented international duet. At the end, I ran over and gave him a huge hug. Between gasps I thanked him. "You pulled me through!" I said.

The audience was standing. They were clapping thunderously. It was a victory — for me, for Mr. Chou, for both of our teams, for both of our countries. And maybe for the world. Indeed, wouldn't the world be a better place if more people could say, **"I want to help you."**

Small Things

One little unshed raindrop
May think itself too small;
Yet, somewhere, a thirsty flower
Awaits its fall.

One little word, unspoken,
May seem too small to say;
But, somewhere, for that one word,
A heart may pray.

—Helen Thomas Allison

The Love Cards
Fanny-Maude Evans

CREAK-CRACK-CREAK. I sat up in bed. *Creak-crack-creak.* The sound came again. What was it? Footsteps in the hall?

Of course not, I thought flicking on the light. It had to be the hardwood boards in the floor contracting in the cool summer night. I looked at the clock — 2:00 A.M. Only eight hours since I'd left my husband at the San Francisco airport, but now it seemed like eight years. He'd be gone two weeks attending a Bible study course in Wisconsin. He'd been gone before but I had always stayed with friends or my daughter.

This time I had chosen to stay at home. The big garden had to be watered, the fruit and vegetables canned and frozen. Besides, I was a little ashamed. Why couldn't a mature woman conquer her fear of noises in the night? I read my Bible. I believed in God. I prayed for His help every day. Yet, somehow, when I awoke in the night, he seemed very far away.

In the morning, I dragged about my work without enthusiasm. I had plenty to do, yet how many more sleepless nights could I survive? Then, in the mail that day, there was a single postcard. When I turned it over, I read a hand-lettered message:

> *As the candle*
> *Lights up the darkness*
> *So shall my darkness*
> *Be lighted by Him.*

A picture of a lighted red candle had been cut from a magazine and pasted beside the words. That was all. No name, no clue as to who had sent it. The postmark didn't help either. Just the impersonal "U.S. Postal Services."

Who would send such a message? Who, besides a few friends and my daughter, knew about my fears?

That night I propped up the card beside my bed and, as I drifted off to sleep, I was still wondering who my unknown friend could be.

Once more at 2:00 A.M., I was awake, and listening to the *creak-creak* in the hall. When I snapped on the light, I saw the card. God could light my darkness. He could give me sleep if I would just trust Him. But I still could not. I tossed and turned until almost dawn.

The next morning there was another card. This time two birds in flight had been pasted beside the verse:

> *As You've cared for*
> *The birds I see*
> *So shall You care*
> *For me.*

Again there was no signature, no clue.

When I went to bed I placed the second card beside the first and read them both before I turned out the light. When the familiar creaks woke me, I sat up and read the cards out loud. Someone, somewhere, knew and cared. Cared enough to remind me that I was not really alone. Whispering a prayer for help in strengthening my faith, I sank again into sleep.

When I heard the mailman in the morning, I didn't really expect to find a new card. But there it was.

> *Beautiful sunrise,*
> *Sunny and gay,*
> *Thank You, Lord,*
> *For another day.*

And it was a sunny day. I even felt like singing as I thought of someone out there who cared enough to keep reminding me of God's love. When my husband phoned that night, I told him about the cards. But they were just as much a puzzle to him as to me.

Now I could hardly wait for the mail. Each morning the postman brought a card with a new verse and its cutout illustration. It seemed almost as if someone could sense my moods and match the message to them.

A week went by and still the cards kept coming. By now I began to wonder if it could possibly be my niece, my nephew's wife who lived in a town nearly a hundred miles away. Could it be this lovely new Christian, now deeply committed to serving her Lord?

She was so busy, though, with her home and her three small boys. Would she take the time to cut out pictures and write verses?

Yet the more I thought about it, the more possible it seemed. I might have mentioned in a letter that I hated to stay alone at night when my husband was away. Had she remembered?

As the cards piled up beside my bed, I spent more and more time in the evening reading them over. I began to sleep through the night, for the creaks in the hall seemed to have vanished.

On the last day before my husband was to come home, there was no card, but an envelope instead, containing a snapshot of my husband and me together. Mounted on double folds of red paper, it opened like a card. Inside, I read:

I have trusted the Lord
To watch over me.
The time has come.
Together we'll be.

And on an extra slip of white paper, beneath the red card:

Thank You, God,
For everything.

I looked at the picture again. Now I knew it *was* my niece, for I recognized the drapes in her living room where we had been together at Christmas — and Carole's husband had been snapping pictures!

I dialed Carole's number and asked her about the cards.

There was a long silence. Then she said, "I didn't really want you to know who sent them. I wanted to do something nobody would know about, just as it says in that verse in the Bible" (Matthew 6:3, 4).

"Oh, Carole," I said, "God was really using you, though. I've learned a lesson I couldn't seem to learn by myself. I think I'll never really be afraid to stay alone again."

And I haven't been afraid. Carole, the "new" Christian, has taught this old one something utterly basic—a true Christian puts her trust in Him always, day *and* night.

Whispers of Love
Eleanor Sass

WHILE ON A GUIDED TOUR of Grand Central Station here in New York City one day, our group was led into a domed forty-foot-square passageway. "This is an acoustical phenomenon," our guide said.

Then he asked a young couple if they would stand in opposite corners facing the wall. "Whisper something to her," he ordered the young man. No one else could hear what the boy said, but I happened to be standing next to the girl. "What did he say?" I asked her. Her face was radiant. "He told me he loved me." Then she turned back to the wall and I saw her whisper her answer: "I love you, too." Only the boy standing in the corner on the opposite side of the passageway could hear her words, meant for him alone.

The next day was Sunday. In church, as I bowed my head to pray before the start of the service, I remembered the scene in Grand Central the day before. "I love you, Father," I whispered.

No one else could hear, but His answer came back to me along the vaulted archways of prayer, words for me alone: "I love you, too, My child."

All day long the sun shone brighter because of that.

The Troublemaker
Phyllis Delikowski

FROM THE FIRST DAY OF CLASS, her tiny figure topped by a mop of jet-black hair and a brilliant red ribbon seemed to exude an air of defiance. Mary rarely participated with the rest of my second-grade church-school group, and then only on her own terms — kicking her neighbor under the table, taking someone's books, pushing, shoving. Nothing I tried, no amount of cajoling or remonstrance, seemed to reach her. At first I felt irritation, then anger. Eventually I decided simply to ignore her.

Yet each week after class I would go home with that red ribbon waving in my mind, taunting me. *Why let it bother you?* I asked myself. *Aside from Mary, the class is going well. You have things under control.* But it was an empty argument, for I could sense that something was missing from that classroom. Something important, something elusive. And I didn't know what it was.

Then one Sunday I gathered my students around me to hear the story of Jesus blessing the children. "After I've read the story," I promised, "we'll act it out." It was a game they loved, pretending we were actually living in the time when Christ was on earth, seeing, hearing and touching Him.

So, after finishing the story, I said, "Now let's go back to the time of Jesus. Close your eyes and imagine it all . . . the color of the sky . . . the warm breeze . . . the feel of grass beneath our bare feet as we gather around Jesus, waiting to be held by Him. There He is! Imagine His eyes, His smile, the sound of His voice as He speaks individually to each one of us. Listen to His magic words . . . "

Crack! I saw Mary's book come crashing down on the unsuspecting head of her neighbor, an amiable little boy named Jeff. A tremendous wave of anger shot through me at the sight. "Mary!" I shouted. "Why did you do that?"

My own voice shocked me. Never before had I screamed at a child in such a way. But my voice rushed on furiously, the words tumbling out of me. "What if Jesus were here right now? What do you think He'd say to you?"

A hush fell over the room. All eyes were fixed on Mary's defiant face. Then a voice spoke, barely a whisper. "I love you." For a moment it seemed as if we really were back with Jesus, and He was speaking to us. But the voice belonged to Jeff. Jeff, the offended one. Jeff, who had heard and understood the magic words of Jesus that we all had been listening for.

Jeff had given us Jesus' answer. And now I had my answer, too. I had closed my heart against Mary for far too long. It was love that was missing from my classroom.

"Yes, Mary," I said, "Jesus does love you." I paused. Was there a hint of softness in those deep brown eyes?

"Mary? I love you, too."

And then, for the first time, Mary smiled.

The Language of Love
Claire Mitchell

I WAS SHOPPING in a drugstore in Washington, D.C., one day when I noticed a small boy taking jars from a low counter and playing "train" with them on the floor. The clerk saw him and shouted, "Leave those things alone; you'll break them." The child turned a puzzled face to the clerk. In that moment I noticed the little boy was not completely normal. After a pause, he again began playing with the items. The clerk scolded him, his voice loud and angry.

Suddenly a girl about seven years old appeared from around the end of the counter, ran to the boy and, dropping on her knees beside him, put an arm about him and began to speak softly. I couldn't hear what she said. But the boy slowly and carefully began to replace the items on the shelf.

The little girl then rose to her feet and faced the clerk. "He doesn't understand when you talk that way," she said. "He understands what I say because I *love* it into him."

"I Choosed You"
Marjorie Holmes

I T'S NO SECRET that I didn't want my fourth child. I was in tears when our family doctor confirmed it. "But I already *have* three children — one of them ready for college. I thought I'd finally have more time for other things I enjoy!"

"Please don't take it like that," he tried to comfort me. "I'm sure this child will be a great blessing to you."

Oh, he says that to all his patients, I thought. *He's just being kind.* But Melanie was a joy and special treasure to all of us from the moment she arrived. And as she grew older she grew in grace, delight and beauty, with a wisdom that at times astonished me. Best of all, she loved the Lord.

I remember a time when she was barely five years old. We were walking past a church, and as she danced along beside me she was chanting a little made-up song: "Oh, oh, oh, I think you are the nicest mommy in the world. Oh, oh, oh, I love you, and you know why? When I was a baby angel in heaven God asked me: 'Look down and see which mother do you choose?' and I said, 'Eenie, meenie, miney-mo, catch a mommy by the toe. If she hollers let her go.' *But I choosed you!*"

It seemed funny at the time; only later did I feel its deeper significance. And even today I sometimes wonder: in the mysteries of creation, isn't it possible there are little souls somewhere just waiting to be born? Perhaps even choosing the parents God wants them to have?

Perhaps someone reading this today has a new life stirring within her. Unexpected, and yes, unwelcome. If you are such a someone, please remember this true story. Such a child can be a tremendous joy and comfort—beyond your wildest dreams. Perhaps there is a tiny angel somewhere who "choosed you" because God wanted it to, a child who will fill a special need in your life as it develops into a beautiful life of its own.

Accept this for the precious gift it is, and be thankful.

"You Love Me"
Elizabeth Sherrill

I HADN'T SEEN David and Marilyn since they retired and moved to Arizona, but through Christmas cards I'd followed their ups and downs. For the past four years, since David was diagnosed as having Alzheimer's disease, I gathered that things had been pretty grim. Two months before a *Guideposts* assignment took me to Phoenix, Marilyn had at last placed him in a nursing home—and that's where she and I were driving now.

"He won't know you," she warned as she parked in front of the Spanish-style building. "He doesn't know the children, anyone."

She was right. There was no recognition in David's eyes as I gripped the passive hand on the arm of the wheelchair.

But he was obviously well cared-for in the clean, cheery facility. It was Marilyn I was concerned about. Nothing on the Christmas cards had communicated the strain on her of these last four years. She was down to ninety-eight pounds and badly stooped with arthritis, yet she was making this twelve-mile trip every day of the week to feed David his noonday meal.

"This is Tib, dear," she told him for the fifth or sixth time. "Remember, we used to be neighbors?"

No response.

"Who's this?" She lifted a framed photograph of their daughter from the dresser. David stared at it, then shook his head.

It was the same with pictures of their son, their grandchildren, their old collie. Marilyn lifted his hands from the chair arms, held them in both of hers and leaned close.

"Who am I, dear?"

That same bemused stare. Then his face brightened. For just a moment he looked like the David I remembered.

"You love me," he said.

They were the only words he spoke during my visit. But what else, I thought, as the plane carried me back east, do we need to know? About one another. About God. When we don't know . . . when we can't understand . . . when we're not sure of anything at all . . . we can still answer him with a joyful cry:

You love me.

PART 5

Forgiveness

Because we are human, even with the most loving of relationships there is need for forgiveness. In relationships, as with roses, we can concentrate on the fragrant blossoms, or we can push the thorns into our hands, which is what we do when we focus on the unkindness of others. Often we learn our first lessons on forgiveness in childhood, when adults demonstrate that their first concern is our welfare rather our mistake. Perhaps the hardest time to forgive is when the very fabric of a marriage is threatened. Yet even there, God can give the power to forgive, and to change and restore both partners.

The Broken Stein

Louise Hunt

"TEACHER, Bobby broke your German dish!" I turned and saw the remnants of my beautiful German stein shattered on the classroom floor.

Grief welled up in me as I put the broken pieces back in the box of keepsakes I had brought to show my sixth graders.

"I should have known better than to bring them," I blurted. But the bell for classes sounded before I could give Bobby the tongue lashing I thought he deserved.

"Fred," I said with forced calmness to another student, "it's your turn to lead the morning exercises."

"Stand," Fred's nasal tones came to me as if in a dream. "Salute." But my mind was not on the flag as the children recited the pledge.

"Bow your heads in prayer," Fred continued. "Almighty God," I mumbled along with the children, "we acknowledge our dependence upon Thee . . . "

Then, like water from an upturned pitcher, my anger suddenly drained from me. And in one of those rare and illuminating moments, I felt a warm glow of compassion for Bobby standing with head bowed, mingled shame and despair on his face — too big a boy to cry.

The class concluded the prayer we repeat each morning . . . "and beg Thy blessing upon us." To myself I added, "and thank You God for forgiveness . . . "

"Bobby, I know you couldn't help it," I said gently as the children finished. "The stein can be mended. Now, won't you help me show the rest of these souvenirs to the class?"

"Sure, Mrs. Hunt," Bobby answered joyfully.

Watching the boy carefully carrying my treasures up and down the aisles I thought, "That stein has done more for me, broken, than it ever could have done in one piece."

The Not Forgotten
Jean Bell Mosley

I TRY TO REMEMBER the details of that long-ago day. They went something like this: Summer was over the land. I was barefoot, maybe seven or eight. The pink zinnias were in bloom. Mama was baking a special cake, my favorite, with little colored pillows of candy embedded in the icing. But as I look back, the cake was not important, nor the zinnias, nor my freed feet.

Desiring some teenage privacy from the rest of the family, my older sister had made a room for herself in a corner of the big log smokehouse. In a swept-out corner she had put a chair, a desk, a clumsy wooden-box bookcase. I could not understand this. In there alone with the old smoky hams and strings of onions and hanks of dried pennyroyal! Why?

If my sister thought she had privacy, I could have told her she didn't, for some plaster had fallen from the chinks between the logs, and if I wanted to, I could see her every move. And from time to time I wanted to.

One day I didn't draw back quickly enough. My sister's shocked eyes bore into mine, at close range. Due report of my behavior was made, and Mama instructed me never to peek again.

But I did. There was another place the plaster was missing, a place where my sister wouldn't be expecting me to peek. All I could ever see that she was doing was reading a book.

This time I was caught, unexpectedly, from the rear, and Mama hauled me off to a place under the big cherry tree. Memory fades here. Was I spanked? Was I scolded? Shamed? Probably.

I do remember that when Mama was through with the "correction," she hugged me and said, "Now let's forget this ever happened." And I also remember the awful sinking feeling I had. I thought Mama would never again love me. I wandered off to the creek, waded awhile. But it wasn't fun. I went to the strawstack, crawled way back into a little cave the cows had made as they ate into it. It was suffocatingly hot, but I stayed for a long time, trying to do some sort of penance, I suppose. I thought about going to an abandoned log cabin about a mile away and staying there the rest of my life. I wished the lump in my throat would go away. I wished it were yesterday or tomorrow. I wished I hadn't disobeyed.

Soon I began to think of that cake Mama had baked. It was high and fluffy, and those little nuggets of sweetness on top! *My* cake. I wondered if dinnertime had come and gone. I could imagine the family gathered around the table, Dad saying, "I'll have another piece of the cake, please," and no one missing me. Not even Mama.

I went back to the house, looked quickly through the screen door. There was the cake, untouched, in the center of the table. I went around to look in a kitchen window, and then another one. Once, I felt sure Mama saw me, but she didn't say anything. I went again to the screen door and stood, this time long enough to be seen.

"Want to lick the icing bowl?" Mama asked, just like she always did.

I stepped inside and stood there by the door, wondering if I shouldn't say something.

"Mama . . . " I began.

"Here, there's a lot left," she said, handing me the bowl and a spoon. She brushed the hair back out of my eyes. I looked into hers. There was no trace of disappointment, anger or disapproval.

"But, Mama," I began again, feeling hot and sticky and throbbing with the necessity to say something more, to get the mighty hurt out of my throat.

"Hurry up," she said. "It'll soon be dinnertime. I want you to set the table."

"Mama, I won't do it again."

"Do what?"

"You know."

"Whatever you're talking about, I've forgotten." She busied herself with the potatoes.

I licked the bowl clean, wondering all the while if it really were possible to forget something like that, not over an hour old. I watched Mama furtively as she sliced the bread, poured the milk. Surely there would be some little telltale sign to show that she remembered my disobedience — a frown, a reference to my wrongdoing. She only smiled and hummed a little tune, just like always.

Yes, I supposed it was possible. My Mama could do anything. Never had I felt so wonderful, so free and airy, so everything-is-all-right.

"Can we use the rose-sprigged dishes?" I asked. They were our Sunday and special-occasion dishes.

Mama looked only a little puzzled. Then, looking around, said, "Why, I suppose so. It's such a pretty day. You'll be careful."

The world, which had stopped for me, now moved on, better than ever. Old Tabby came out from behind the cookstove, humped her back and curled up in a spot of sunshine before the opened door. I picked a bouquet of pink zinnias for the table.

Over the years, Mama may have indeed forgotten that incident, but I haven't and hope I don't. It was my first glorious experience of what total forgiveness is like. Had she not demonstrated it, it may have been harder for me in later life to believe it could be done, harder for me to reexperience the ineffable peace, the joyous uplift that comes from knowing that confessed transgressions are forgotten by One who *really can* do anything, who can take these wrongdoings and hurl them into oblivion, which is somewhere as far as the east is from the west, the heavens from the earth. Rejoice!

Abounding in Love
Patricia Houck Sprinkle

HOW DO YOU DEAL with friends who disappoint you, children who disobey you, spouses who forget their promises and co-workers who fail to follow through on important assignments? Are you, like me, usually concerned with what is "fair" or "right"?

One night as I read Psalm 103:8-10(RSV), I seemed to hear God say, "This is the way *I* deal with those who let *Me* down."

The Lord is merciful and gracious . . . How often do I show mercy — compassion, clemency — to my children? My spouse? My friends or co-workers? Do I speak and act graciously to them when they have disappointed me?

Slow to anger and abounding in steadfast love . . . "Abounding" means "filled to the very brim with." Can I be filled with enough love to give up my own quick temper and respond to others with steadfast, "never-failing" love?

He will not always chide . . . God is no nag . . . *Nor will He keep His anger for ever.* God holds no grudges. Can I give up my own nagging and grudges?

He does not deal with us according to our sins, nor requite us according to our iniquities. Can I learn to be gentle in dealing with the faults of others? Can I overlook their flaws?

God's way of dealing with people who disappoint Him is not my most natural way. It's harder. But it's also a far better way.

A Very Small Prayer

Teach me to know this, O Lord!
No matter what else I may do,
Whenever I fail to love, I am wrong.

— Simons Roof

How to Forgive
Jane Braddock[*]

OUR THREE TEEN-AGERS had scattered to separate activities of their own for the evening, and my husband, Tom, and I were enjoying a rare meal out all by ourselves. The pizza with hot, savory cheese and garlic bits sprinkled on top was a mouth-watering treat. Being alone with Tom was extraspecial too, since I had just come home from a four-day trip, taking my elderly parents to visit my sister.

"Anything happen while I was gone?" I asked Tom.

"Nothing out of the ordinary," he said. "The kids and I managed just fine."

But then he made a casual remark that turned the pizza into tasteless cardboard.

"I did call Susan one day to invite her to lunch," he said.

"You did *what?*" I could hear my voice, strident and loud in the suddenly too-quiet pizza parlor. My stomach twisted into a cold knot and my hands fell to the napkin in my lap. I pulled the wedding ring from my finger and dropped it into my purse, fighting for control.

Memories came flooding to the surface of my consciousness, memories I'd thought gone forever . . . vivid pictures of Tom and Susan going dancing together while I stayed home with the kids . . . mental images of the two of them playing footsies at Friday night dinner and

---

[*]Name has been changed.

bridge get-togethers. Pictures changed to thoughts as I remembered in quick succession the lies and denials Tom used for cover-ups. Even though I was convinced he was never completely unfaithful, I knew the desire had been there. Was this desire surfacing again?

My bitter reveries were interrupted as Tom went on matter-of-factly. "I called Susan for lunch, but she had other plans. No big deal. Nothing happened."

"Nothing happened? What did you *expect* to happen? Why did you call her? I thought that was all finished — buried!" The accusing questions hurled themselves from my lips — ugly, condemning.

"Oh, come on, Jane," Tom implored. "I only asked her out for lunch. If there'd been anything to it, would I have told you about it?"

With the knuckles of a clenched fist, I wiped hard at the tears coursing down my cheeks. My mouth quivered with fury as I spat out the venom erupting inside me. "You called that — that woman when I was gone! You dug up the past! You lusted!" The loud beat of the now blaring jukebox matched the hate pulsing inside me.

Tom's voice was almost a whisper. "I think you're making this into something it's not. Slow down. Back off . . . "

But I couldn't stop. Fear and fury were in motion, along with tearing memories of five years ago when we had been on the brink of divorce because of Susan and other problems. Then we had met Jesus, becoming new creatures, entering into *holy* matrimony after fifteen years of pagan marriage. But now this. Every cell of my body was shaken, and my anger was coupled with a growing hurt so deep I could hardly speak.

"How could you *do* it, Tom? You're supposed to *love* me."

"I don't know why," Tom shrugged. "Lonely, I guess. It just happened. I didn't think it was so wrong — at the time." His big brown eyes were thoughtful, searching mine. "Guess I haven't arrived at sainthood yet, huh? I'm human, fallible. The Lord's still molding this hunk of clay. But I'm sorry. I *do* love you. Will you forgive me, Jane?" His right hand slid across the table, reaching for mine.

I pretended not to see. My head was spinning. I had to get out. Somehow my feet took me to the car, and I drove blindly away. But there was no place to go, no place to hide, and after a while I came back to the house. My ranting spent, I wrapped myself in a cloak of martyrdom and went straight to bed.

Moments later, Tom joined me. "Do you want to have our prayer tonight, Jane?"

"No!" There was no need for him to think he could persuade me to seek reconciliation.

"Okay, Jane." But then he went on to pray aloud. "Father, I have done wrong. I confess that to You as sin and ask Your forgiveness. In Jesus' name. Amen."

Well, God might forgive him, but I couldn't. Shaken with sobs, I turned my back. I knew I wasn't supposed to let the sun go down on my wrath, but how could I help it?

A million hours later, it was morning. My head ached terribly, my stomach churned. Worse yet, Tom had slept like a baby. He was the one who should be suffering, not I.

Seething with resentment, I began my Saturday chores. As I shoved the vacuum viciously into corners that had been neglected for a long time, I began complaining about Tom to the Lord. Silently, He reminded me that weeks earlier, in our Sunday school class, all the members had agreed to pray for one another on a regular basis. And this was the day I was supposed to pray for Tom! Until now, I'd thought that praying for one another was a good idea. But how could I make myself pray for my husband when he'd treated me like a— like a—

"Come on, Lord," I found myself saying, "if I can't forgive him, how am I going to pray for him?"

A Scripture I'd learned long ago came at me from somewhere deep inside. "Pray for them which despitefully use you" (Luke 6:28).

Pray for them which despitefully use you. It was too specific to ignore. I had let the sun go down on my wrath and suffered the consequences. My head was still throbbing with them. I couldn't afford to be disobedient again. I certainly didn't feel like praying for Tom, but I did it anyway.

"Lord, bless Tom who despitefully used me. Lord, bless Tom who despitefully used me. Lord, bless Tom who despitefully used me."

It sounded more like a cursing than a prayer, but I said the words many times that day. Tom was at home, but I took pains to stay away from him. Though we ate lunch together, I spoke only when he spoke to me first, and I made every word icy, deliberately trying to spoil his day.

I didn't have to try to spoil mine. It was absolute hell. My whole being ached with resentment. Late in the afternoon, I sat stiffly in a chair in the corner of the den, pretending to read. When Tom walked in and sat down across the room, I let my magazine fall to my lap. I noticed that I had been holding it upside down.

"All right, Jane. It's no use. I've tried to work, but I can't get anything done. I know you haven't forgiven me. It's driving me crazy."

I was delighted to hear that he was suffering. It was the best thing that had happened all day. I opened my mouth to make a nasty comeback, not to say the words that came out:

"I know, Tom. I'm sorry. I forgive you right now."

Tom's mouth — and mine — hung open in amazement. Where had *that* came from? Even as I sat there in shocked surprise, a strange — and wonderful — thing happened. From the top of my head right down to the tip of my toes, I felt all the anger and resentment draining out of me. It was as if I were being washed, made clean from bitterness. More amazing still, in place of the anger and ugliness I'd felt, there was a deep, real trusting love for Tom! I couldn't tell him so right then — I couldn't have told anybody anything. I was so overwhelmed, so awestruck by the change in me, that I could only sit there. Tom seemed to know without my saying another word, though. His eyes met mine, the familiar grin I loved so much spread across his face, and I saw his Adam's apple bob up and down as he swallowed the lump in his throat.

The tears began to roll as I went to fish my wedding ring from my pocketbook; they were refreshingly cool, bathing my hot, dry eyes with soothing rivers of love. The next sound I heard was Tom's joyful whistle accompanying the purposeful ringing of his hammer. He'd gone back to work on the new kitchen cabinets he was building for me in the basement.

Taking my Bible from the shelf where it had lain neglected all day, I curled up in a chair to thumb through it, asking the Holy Spirit to show me what had happened. How could I be so angry, so full of resentment one moment—and so at peace, so filled with love the next? What had caused the change? I certainly hadn't willed it. I hadn't even asked God to change my attitude, so I couldn't take any credit for it. Where had it come from?

There was the answer, plain as day, in two Scriptures I knew well but had never put together in my mind till then. The first one, in the book of James, said, "But be ye doers of the word, and not hearers only, deceiving your own selves" (James 1:22).

No matter how I had felt about it, I had "done" the Word that said I was to pray for the one who despitefully used me.

The other Scripture was the beautiful passage in Isaiah, telling that it is not only the rain and snow which accomplish the purpose for which God had sent them, but better yet, "So shall my word be that goeth forth out of my mouth: it shall not return unto me void, but it shall accomplish that which I please" (Isaiah 55:11).

These Scriptures, taken together, seemed to be saying to me that
by doing His Word, I had returned it to Him so it
could accomplish its purpose in my life, restoring
me to a right relationship with Tom—and
with God Himself. What could I
say but "Thank You, Lord,
for Your powerful Word!
Thank You!
Thank
You!"

Thorns or Roses?
Marjorie Holmes

M{Y HUSBAND} was arranging the roses on the table when I came downstairs after a restless night. Our first sweet red buds opening, and one the color of sunrise, in full bloom. I knew he had cut them early to surprise me. For I had scarcely slept, tormented by painful words and thoughts that, no matter how I pleaded, my mind refused to stop.

"Oh, how beautiful!" Comforted, I plunged my face into the fragrant bouquet. But turning to start breakfast, I asked, "Why is it that when we're young it's the happy things that keep us awake? At least mine were: a compliment, a wonderful date, winning a contest. But when we get older why is it usually the worries, the things that hurt? Like being so let down by Jane?"

"I don't know, honey, but it's true," he said. "Maybe because we're disappointed. Our dreams seldom turn out quite as rosy as we painted them. People fail us. Instead of remembering the good things, we're more likely to wrestle with the problems." He put his hand on my shoulder. "But try not to let it matter. Jane has been such a dear friend so long. She hasn't really changed; you've just seen something in her you didn't recognize before. Think of the wonderful times you've had together, how much you mean to each other."

"But she has hurt me!" I cried.

"Then don't hurt yourself any more by dwelling on it." He took the full-blown rose from the vase and handed it to me. "Look at this rose. You can see its beautiful colors, you can enjoy its fragrance — but it still has thorns. If you want to, you can press them into your flesh until you bleed. Thoughts are like that, they can be beautiful or painful. You can make your very heart bleed with your thoughts."

"I've *tried* not to think about it," I pleaded. "What can I do to make them stop?"

"Forgive her and love her," he said simply.

I gasped. It seemed impossible, but oddly my heart felt lighter. And when I had prayed about it, I knew he was right. Wasn't that what Jesus would do for me?

Are You All Right?
Aletha Jane Lindstrom

I'LL NEVER FORGET one summer day when I was eight and my mother sent me out for milk. She wanted it in a hurry, so I rode my bike to the grocery store down the road. Carrying the glass quart bottle in my hand as I steered home, I hit a bump, and I, and the milk, went sprawling. The bottle shattered and milk spilled everywhere.

My knee was scraped up and I hurt all over, but I was even more afraid of being yelled at when I got home. My family didn't exactly have extra money to waste, and it was just before dinner. But when I wheeled my bike into our yard, my father rushed toward me. "Are you all right?" he asked, seeing my forlorn face. "Did you get cut?" Only after carefully checking me over did we go to clean up the glass.

When my son Tim was eight years old, he wanted to help by feeding the horses when his dad was sick. As he carried a big armful of hay through the gate, he forgot to close it behind him, and all the horses escaped. When he told me, I wanted to scream! "Tim, how c—" I began. But a picture rose to mind of my father's face. He'd had to make a split-second choice: to yell at me for my mistake or to react toward me with love and concern. I had to go out and get the horses back, but I had something else I had to do first.

I took a deep breath and reached my hand out
to touch Tim's tear-stained cheek.
"Are you all right, Son?"
I asked.

PART 6

Encouragement

Love notices when another person needs encouragement. Sometimes it may be just a word, a note, or a letter that lets the other person know they are thought about and cared for. Sometimes encouragement includes a word of discipline spoken in love. But always love acts — to bring joy, hope, faith into another's dark times.

Blossom by the Levee
Luana Thiel Jambois

CLEMILLE WAS HIS NAME. Sandy-haired and freckled he was, with spindly arms and legs protruding from an unironed shirt and frayed pants that were several sizes too small for him; and he moved in the languorous manner that spelled out instant trouble. But his eyes. God help us, those eyes were gray and filled with searching; and that was why he had condescended to come at all.

I had never taught school before. My palms were sweating as I looked at the young faces before me, but the children were friendly and expectant. All but Clemille. Old eyes, his seemed, in a child's head.

"Dearest Lord," I prayed as I went on with roll call, "help me to help this one."

I congratulated the children for coming. Religious weekend class was entirely voluntary, and they could have been playing in the bayou country's tree-shaded sunlight rather than sitting in a stuffy room with me for two and a half hours. I was a city girl and I hadn't the faintest idea how difficult it was for most of them to come, or I'd have said I appreciated that, too.

They were pleased. They leaned forward, smiling, their eyes shifting to Clemille.

He stood up, rocking back on his heels. His voice in its river-road accent was thick with insolence. "You from here? I never saw you around."

I flushed, but then told them about myself. "Introduce yourselves," I said, "starting with Clemille, since he's already standing." Gleeful grins from all but Clemille. Their smiles said I'd won that round and today the classroom was mine.

Clemille thawed a bit. "Got twelve sisters and brothers. Everybody knows where we live." His thumb jerked toward the direction of the river. "You ever been on River Road, teacher? It runs alongside the river." The class laughed.

"Thanks for telling me," I sassed back. "I don't think I'd have missed it."

Grinning broadly, he sat down, and I congratulated myself.

I needn't have, because the weekly hassle between Clemille and me became one of the features of each class.

I had read that when a child misbehaves, he is searching for attention. So I appointed Clemille eraser-cleaner, blackboard cleaner, paper-taker-upper. It didn't make a dent in him.

Then one day I stumbled on the idea of asking if anyone knew any Catholic hymns. Clemille's face brightened. "I do," he said and was up to the front of the class, singing "Rock of Ages" before I could say another word. He'd learned it, he told me later, at a little Baptist mission on the levee. His voice was clear and true as he sang, but the other children snickered behind their hands. This was pre-ecumenism, and Protestant hymns weren't Catholic hymns, no matter how inspiring.

I frowned and called for silence, as he wavered to a stop, abashed and suddenly speechless. "How many of you children got up to sing? Clemille was singing for God, and singing is the best prayer there is!" I glared at them. "If Clemille will forgive us, we'll listen to the rest of the song and try to sing it with him. That is, if he'll teach us."

He looked at me blankly.

Please, Clemille, I prayed, *please don't give up now.*

He hitched up his pants. Nothing in the world ever seemed as courageous to me as the skinny, tawny-haired boy, planting his feet, staring the class down, and singing "Rock of Ages."

The next week I mimeographed some new hymns for the class to learn. I chose Clemille as song leader, dividing his other chores among the children. He gloried in it. Gone was the surliness, those old-man eyes. He was first in class, waiting for me in the morning, as avid to learn about God as a parched man was to drink.

But, Clemille being Clemille, that wasn't the end of his problems. One day, when I arrived home from my weekly grocery shopping, my neighbor waved. "A boy left a bag for you on the side steps," she called.

In a small paper bag, I found flowers. How lovely they were! I knew instinctively that they were from Clemille. I thanked him profusely the following Saturday, and he blushed with pleasure.

The next week the bag was larger. Again I thanked him. This time, though, I drove past his house on the old shell-and-gravel road. With a sinking feeling, I realized that what I had suspected was true. Outside his house a slatted porch swing moved gently in the river breeze. A family grew there — but not one flower. Over everything was a pall of clinging, grayish shell dust. Even the grass was coated with it. No flower could have grown there.

There was an enormous supermarket grocery bag on the side steps the next week. My neighbor didn't have to say, "That boy was there again."

I took the bag and opened it on the kitchen table. Camellias and azaleas, the dew not dried yet on their petals—roses, daisies, larkspurs, lilies, gardenias.

I buried my face in the flowers, seeing Clemille's face the first time I'd met him, and how he'd changed. Dear God, how could I, a religious teacher, accept these flowers, knowing he'd stolen them, without trying to teach him, without risking that eager aliveness in him I'd been so happy about. My house was filled with flowers because of this strange, half-wild boy who'd grown so suddenly tame; and I prayed that I'd know how to tell him so I wouldn't hurt him.

Next Saturday I pinned the last of the camellias on my dress. Clemille beamed at me across the rows when he saw it there.

"Yes, ma'am?" He'd given me that accolade too. Saying "ma'am" was a big concession.

"The flowers, Clemille. My house was filled with them. They were so beautiful! How can I thank you?"

His gesture was large and sweeping. "That's all right." Smiling, he turned to leave.

"Wait!" I swallowed. "Clemille, I love to see flowers blooming outside too."

He looked puzzled. I hadn't hurt him, but I hadn't helped him, either. I forced myself to start again.

"Clemille, sometimes we take things that belong to other people without knowing what it means to them. When I plant flowers, I watch each new change that happens, from seed to sprout. I even look forward to seeing each flower. Most people do that. They plant their flowers to see them grow." I held my breath. "Clemille, we should never take other people's hopes away from them. Not even when they're flowers."

I didn't have to say anymore. The deed was done. He hung his head and twisted his foot. "Yes, ma'am."

"Clemille, look at me." I grabbed his hand. "Oh, Clemille! That's the first time in my life that my house was filled with flowers! And you gave them to me!"

He grinned. "Okay. See you next week, teach." He'd forgiven me. He'd accepted what I'd tried to teach him. Till the end of that term, he never wavered. Afterward, he'd come back and visit me in my new classes sometimes.

Years later, after I'd moved back to the city, I visited that country town. Clemille, I heard, had married young and settled down early. "A good boy," they called him. His relatives had hit reform school, even jail, but not Clemille.

Like those growing flowers he had picked, bursting from precious seeds, Clemille had himself, under the sunshine of love, blossomed. And how blessed I was to behold the beauty of it.

The Homely Twin
Linda Ching Sledge

BARBARA WAS THE HOMELY TWIN. Although I tried not to compare the ten-year-old sisters, I couldn't help being astonished by the contrast between them. Barbara was chubby, Betty was slim; Barbara was painfully shy, Betty was assertive and outgoing. Barbara had straight brown hair. Betty's golden curls were the envy of the neighborhood girls. Whenever company came, Betty would smile and start a conversation. Barbara would stare stonily ahead. Neighbors thought Barbara rude.

Driving home from the train station one day, my husband noticed Barbara walking up the hill ahead of us. "Don't bother waving," I told him. "She'll just ignore you."

My husband rolled down his window and grinned. "Hi, Barbara!" he yelled and waved at her. As I predicted, she gave no response.

"See? I told you," I said.

"Look back," replied my husband, watching the child in the rear-view mirror.

I turned and saw Barbara shyly wiggling two fingers at us.

"That little girl needs someone to wave at her," my husband said, "because she doesn't think anyone wants to."

An End to Hopelessness
Eric Thomas

AFTER MOM'S STROKE, we didn't know how much she'd be able to recover. She was so impaired we had to send her to a rehabilitation hospital. At first, she made so little progress we were afraid she'd have to enter a nursing home.

Then, suddenly, after three months of therapy, Mom was well enough to come home and live with us. The day before her discharge, my wife and I sat in on her therapy sessions, and it was then that I discovered some of the secrets behind Mom's drastic improvement.

The physical and occupational therapists who helped my mother used gentle encouragement, saying, "Edith, this is important for you," when she got discouraged. There was the young speech therapist who would tease and joke my mother into practicing her speaking, yet treated her humanly. In fact, the tone and words of every member of the team expressed, in a word — *love.*

These people who cared for Mom showed me something new. I may not have time to give everyone I know the kind of intense love that the rehabilitation team gave my mother. But I can at least try to inject some love into someone's day every day, whether it's helping my sons with their homework or persuading a work colleague that he can handle an intimidating job. After all, I've learned something about love. It can make thriving life out of hopelessness.

It Will Get Better
Marion Bond West

DOROTHY MILLER had been a nun. She gave it up to become a mother. Never married, she adopted ten severely retarded, brain-damaged, emotionally disturbed children. Doctors insisted one underweight girl would only be a vegetable. Dorothy proved them wrong. There were spina bifida children, Down's syndrome and other diagnoses I didn't even begin to understand.

Dorothy ran a tight ship. There was firm discipline, along with unrestrained love. No pity was allowed. Dorothy taught the children to help one another. It was amazing to watch their feeding, toothbrushing and getting-into-leg-braces routine.

One Sunday, after I was newly widowed, my teenage sons and I were having a heated argument while eating in a restaurant. I ended up crying, leaving my food untouched. Just then Dorothy and her brood came in — smiling, laughing, limping, some pushing wheelchairs. She saw me and waved, and they got seated. One of her boys kept watching me. Finally, he came over, patted my shoulder, looked me directly in the eyes and said with a slight speech impediment and a perfect smile, "I tan see ooh having hard time. It will det better."

"Thank you," I responded, greatly encouraged, half laughing, half crying. He was right. It did get better. I still marvel over the compassion Dorothy Miller instills in each of her remarkable children. It's something I can learn — and be reminded of — from them.

A Letter Came Today

Just a plain white homey letter came today
From a long-time friend a continent away.
Strange, I thought, that such a simple thing
Could so neatly turn a winter day to spring.

— Robert Caldwell

The Note
Linda Ching Sledge

WHEN I FIRST STARTED teaching college in New York City, I admired a veteran professor named Jim. He was a happy-go-lucky person, until he lost a valued promotion. Then I watched him slide into depression. I wanted to make Jim feel better, but I didn't know what to say. Though I sympathized with his pain, I had never gone through what he had. So I did nothing. Finally, out of cowardice, I wrote Jim a note. I avoided the issue of his promotion and focused on his fine teaching. Then I slipped the note in his mailbox, hoping I hadn't done the wrong thing.

The next day, as I was tiptoeing past Jim's office, his door opened. I looked up to find Jim's face beaming at me. "Thanks," he said. "That note was just the comfort I needed. You did exactly the right thing."

It's so hard to know what is the "right thing" to do when friends are depressed or grieving. Yet looking back, here's what I learned from my experience with Jim.

1. *Don't* give in to your own indecision.
2. *Do* something as soon as possible.
3. *Don't* give advice unless asked.
4. *Do* listen with patience and sympathy.
5. *Don't* tell your friend that you know exactly how he or she feels. You don't, exactly.
6. *Do* something practical and tangible. Treat him or her to a meal, give a small gift, write an upbeat note.

PART 7

Generosity

Love loves to give — to spend itself for others. It is the opposite of the tight-fisted miser, who focuses only on self and wants to hoard possessions. "Love . . . ever stands\With open hands," as John Oxenham wrote. Where there is need, love gives what it has, whether that is little or much. But love also gives just for the sheer joy of loving — and giving.

The Spendthrift
Harriet Hutchings

AFTER A PARTICULARLY hectic summer of being a taxi service for our four children and picking up after them, something happened to open my eyes to a new dimension of being a mother.

Our second son's birthday is in the first week of September and is always right in the middle of all the flurry of going back to school. That year, when Bill asked for money instead of presents, I can remember thinking how much easier it would be to fill that request than to do the usual hunting through crowded stores for gifts. Eleven is a hard year for finding just the right presents anyway.

So, on his birthday Bill received a few things, but in the cards from friends and relatives, he got the grand total of fourteen dollars. For someone who was still getting a thirty-five-cent allowance, that looked like a small fortune!

His birthday fell on a Sunday. The next morning he happily rode his bike to school. Since our family puts birthday cards on the mantel for a week or so to be admired — it makes the celebration last longer — I paused in front of Bill's cards that morning and chuckled at the humor in the one from his older brother. Then I noticed that all the money tucked inside the cards the night before had been removed. My first thought was, *Oh, he's taken it to school and he'll either lose it or spend it foolishly on the way home.* But then I told myself, "It's his money and he must learn how to handle it."

During the day I forgot about it. With my five-year-old I shopped for groceries on the way home from his kindergarten class. Then we read a few books together while waiting for the others to come home. My daughter and oldest son came in and received the usual noisy welcome from the dog, and after some cookies and milk, hurried off on their own pursuits. I asked them if they had seen Bill coming home, and they told me he had ridden toward the main street and the stores.

I knew it. That darn money was burning a hole in his pocket. With his sweet tooth, I could imagine him filling up on candy and ice cream and probably treating all his friends. His father would ask why I had allowed him to take all the money to school. I could feel family storm clouds brewing.

About half an hour before my husband was due home, I heard a bicycle coming down the driveway. It was moving slowly because Bill was balancing a high shopping bag on the handlebars. Well, whatever he bought, it was *big*. Breathlessly and with much rustling of paper, he came through the door.

"Hey, where is everybody?" Hearing the commotion, his brothers and sister tore themselves away from the television cartoons and came into the kitchen. "Where's Dad?" Bill asked. I told him that his father was not home yet, and Bill answered, "Well, I can't wait."

Looking for all the world like an old peddler opening his pack, he began to take out his purchases. "Here," he said, presenting his sister with a doll, "this is for you." Next, out came a shiny red dump truck for his little brother and a model airplane for our older boy. "I got Dad this little Civil War cannon so he would remember our trip to Gettysburg. See, he can put it on his desk.

"Now wait, there's more," Bill said, and diving into the bag, pulled out an enormous stuffed green frog. "Mother, this is for you." I could feel the tears welling up in my eyes. I had seen that frog and admired it one day while shopping for school supplies with the children. "What a happy frog," I remembered saying. "I'd like to sit him on my bed." I had even picked it up and given it a hug because it was that kind of a frog.

Bill looked at me anxiously. "Hey, don't look sad. This is your happy frog."

"I'm not sad. Those are joyful tears dripping on him. Oh, thank you, Bill." Suddenly I remembered. "What did you get for yourself?"

"Nothing," he replied. "But that's all right. That's why I wanted the money. I wanted to have enough money of my very own to buy each of you a present, and I did."

Supper that night was an especially happy meal. As we said grace I thanked God for each of my children and for my husband's love. Bill beamed under our thanks and knew the joy of giving.

The cannon sits on my husband's desk in his office and the frog still perches on my pillow. In the twelve years that have passed since then, it has lost an eye and its nose is squashed a little flat from children leaning on him, but it is a happy frog. Whenever I wonder if I am loved, I can look at it and feel the gift of love my son gave us all.

Love Ever Gives

Love ever gives —
Forgives — outlives —
And ever stands
With open hands.
And while it lives,
It gives.
For this is Love's prerogative
To give, and give, and give.

—John Oxenham

Night of the Big Storm
Deon Dodd

I COULD FEEL THE STORM BUILDING while I worked in the barn that Sunday afternoon. I'd been fixing the tractor for Monday's plowing and when I headed for the house, black clouds were gathering in the northeast.

I stopped on the porch for a minute and looked across this part of New Mexico where you can see for three days. I felt pretty good. Glenda and I with our little boy had just moved onto this place after working for other people. We had put ourselves on the line for 480 acres, borrowed money for a tractor and sunk what little cash we had in a down payment on sixty-nine head of cattle — forty-nine steers for summer pasture and twenty cows and calves. The cattle, plus growing corn, weren't enough to hire help for, but sure were enough to run your tongue out keeping up.

I felt mighty proud of it all after being on my own for only a few years. Our place wasn't big but I had done it all by myself. It showed what a man could do if he put his mind to it and worked hard enough. I stepped inside, grabbed Glenda around the waist and swung her around. "What's to eat for your rancher husband?" I asked.

That night the storm hit. First came rabbit-killing hailstones, then that black sky opened. Wind howled down hundreds of miles of open country.

By about 10:00 P.M. we could see by lightning flashes that water was building up in the draw, a large gully into which the state road dipped. Then our friends Dick and Carolyn DeVaney knocked at our door. They couldn't get through the draw. As the women talked, Dick and I watched the road. Soon headlights built up around it. It was Memorial Day weekend and folks who'd been picnicking up north at Ute Lake were trying to get home.

We put on slickers. Dick loaded his family into my pickup truck and we pulled it across the draw with my tractor. He took them on home along with the people he picked up from some of the stalled cars. Then he came straight back and helped me haul other cars through the draw.

Folks came into both of our houses to dry off and Glenda and Carolyn kept coffeepots going.

Once while we were pulling a car, Dick yelled, "Man, your lake really lit up with that last flash of lightning!"

What he called a lake is really a dry bed of about ten acres of mesquite grass and black bottom which floods easily.

Finally, about 2:00 A.M., things were pretty well under control. Dick went home and I fell into bed.

Next morning I awoke feeling groggy. Glenda, up fixing breakfast, looked through the window and said she thought she could see a dead calf down by the lake.

"Well," I sighed, pulling on my boots, "maybe there'll be a couple or three." That's not unusual in a storm like that. I drank my coffee, got into the pickup and headed down to the lake.

There *was* a dead calf. And behind it lay a steer — then another and another! Dead cattle were scattered everywhere, in the mud, in the lake. Half-buried in the mud was a bull I had borrowed. I stumbled from the pickup truck in a daze.

When I finished counting, fifty-eight of my sixty-nine head were gone. From the burns on their hides, I figured they had been bunched along the wire fence that crossed the lake when lightning struck. I was ruined.

When I got back to the house, neighbors had gathered. I couldn't say much; I just walked into the house and slumped down at the table. Glenda kept busy baking cookies she had promised for the vacation

Bible school at our church. She had helped bottle-feed many of those calves. Some friends sat with us. Mostly I just stared into my coffee.

That afternoon I drove into town to see my insurance agent. I knew my small policy wouldn't cover this. But I just had to ask anyway.

Of course it didn't and I headed back home in a daze. The sun was low and telephone-pole shadows cut black slices across the highway. I felt a bitterness begin to eat into me. Here I'd been out helping other folks and this thing happened to me. I was just about wiped out. Who was looking out for me?

I pulled into our yard and sat at the wheel for a moment. But then, as I climbed out of the car, I could feel something different. I looked around. There in my corral stood a strange steer.

A neighbor leaned on the rail. "C'mon," he called, "I'll help you brand it."

I couldn't say anything. I walked into the barn to get my DOD iron, my hands shaking. As we were fixing to brand the steer, a truck rattled into the yard with a calf in back. From the truck another neighbor yelled, "You may as well brand this one too."

A big lump came up into my throat.

For the next two weeks they came — friends, neighbors, even strangers — with calves, steers and cows, twenty-six of them. Up until now Glenda and I hadn't cried. Now we could hardly keep our eyes dry.

The phone would ring. "Hey, Deon, I got an ol' dwarf calf in my pasture. Would you take it off my hands?" When I'd arrive, there'd be a fine animal.

People, I never did learn who, paid on my gas bill. Another man called and said, "I got a tractor loose and ready to go. Where do you want me to plow?" When I talked to the owner of that borrowed bull, he said, "What bull?" Then he gave me two calves.

At the ranchers and farmers livestock auction they auctioned off a calf seventeen times and put the $1575 it brought into the bank for us. In the meantime, a special account was opened in our name at the local bank. In about three weeks this account grew to $1400. Talk about neighbors!

Calls and letters came in from all over the country from strangers who had read about our loss.

Glenda and I could hardly believe it. Thanks to all the good folks who helped us, we're back to near normal now. And I know there's no real way to express my appreciation except to hope that I'm near when the next fellow needs help for I sure aim to give it.

But a lot more happened to me than just this. When I'm out alone on my tractor or riding through the cattle, I do a lot of thinking about it.

Why did God let it happen? I know it was for a reason. And I know one thing for sure. It did change me. I'm not the independent type I once was. I know that nobody ever does it all by himself in this world.

Now I know that whatever happens, God's hand is in it. And even if I don't know why, I can rest assured He has good reason. I don't know all the things I should know yet, but I do know that if I keep close to Him and try to do His will, I'll keep finding answers the rest of the days of my life.

The Gifts

Yet still in my heart and bright as an ember
Is the memory sweet of quiet September.
Quiet September, when the lamp's amber core
Revealed Mother sewing, building her store:
Gifts for the lonely, gifts for the poor,
For her own large brood and the child at the door.
Oh, always, always will I remember
The beginning of Christmas in quiet September.

— Alice Thurston

The Forgotten Prisoner
Merlin L. Hershberger

ODAY WE CELEBRATED Christ's birthday here in prison and I believe He was with us.

There are ten men working in the same department with me. Ten men, whose crimes were as varied and different as the men themselves. Yet, most of these men are intelligent and understanding.

As Christmas week began, all of us were eagerly looking forward to the Christmas packages which would be arriving from home. For they are the symbol of the love of our families, and our hope for the future. Nothing is more important to a prisoner than to know that someone still cares.

With the arrival of the first packages, there were more smiles, perhaps a little more kindness in our hearts; the problems of prison life were put aside temporarily. This held true for every prisoner except one; and that one man threatened our entire Christmas.

Paul is twenty-six years of age and well liked by all of us. He could usually be counted upon to cheer up the rest of us when prison doldrums crept into us. But Paul had not been receiving mail lately. He offered various excuses for this; his father traveled a lot, thus making writing hard . . . his brother couldn't write letters too well . . . his sister had recently married, and everyone knows how busy a new bride can be . . .

But Paul was certain he would receive a package. They would remember him—at least on Christmas.

We, who worked with Paul, knew what kind of a person he was—full of life and with a heart as big as Christmas itself—we were sure that out there someone would love him enough to remember.

Monday came and went, as did Tuesday and Wednesday. Only two days until Christmas. Paul was now the only one in our prison unit without a package.

By three o'clock, Friday afternoon, the effervescence of Christmas was dead in our department. Where before there had been smiling faces, there were now only scowls.

Paul sat at his work desk now, trying to be oblivious to everything. His eyes were as dull as dirty glass. All of us could see despair and hate being manufactured.

We knew how he felt. Hadn't we at times gone through the same discouragement as mail failed to arrive for us when expected.

Then, without plan or scheme or direction, men began sneaking back to their cells. Soon, in a secluded corner of our department, there accumulated a pile of candy, cigarettes and miscellaneous gifts from the Christmas packages of all these men.

A suitable box appeared. Someone produced a Christmas card. It was inscribed simply: "To you Paul, our friend."

We picked up the package and, a little apprehensively, laid it before Paul, none of us quite sure how it would be received.

Surprised, Paul picked up the card and read it. There was an awkward silence. The air seemed to be charged with an undefinable power; you could feel it as surely as an electrical shock. Of this I am certain; in that moment there seemed to be something more in that room than men and furniture.

Slowly Paul raised his head, and his voice choked with emotion: "I can't pretend that this package takes the place of the one I didn't receive, but of one thing I am sure, it's a better package. It's better because this package represents all you could give. It has come from your hearts. It's the most expensive present ever given to me."

Then, aware for the first time of his tears, he brushed them aside and in an almost inaudible voice said: "Thank you."

It was surprising how many of the so-called "hardened criminals" developed serious head colds.

And so it was that at 3:45 this afternoon, some of us learned just what Christmas should mean—a lesson so often forgotten—that we can truly keep only that which we give away.

Thy Brother

Share with him thy bread of blessing,
Sorrow's burden share;
When thy heart enfolds a brother,
God is there.

— Theodore Chickering Williams

Giving with Imagination
Marilyn Moore

A YOUNG MAN in New York gives mittens to the street people he meets on his walk to work. A housewife takes books to the children of families camping under a highway in Salt Lake City. A boy in Philadelphia collects blankets for the homeless.

I'm inspired by the imagination of these people. In a world that hasn't found a way to care for its own, in cities that haven't enough room for the homeless, these people have found new ways to respond to human need.

Perhaps they were inspired by the innkeeper in Bethlehem. His city's streets were choked with strangers seeking shelter. His inn was full. If he turned his back on Joseph and his pregnant wife, none would blame him. Certainly the shortage of shelter in his city wasn't *his* fault. And yet his imagination spoke to him: *I have this stable. It's warm from the heat of the animals, with sweet-smelling hay for a bed and a manger to cradle a newborn child. It's not much, and yet . . .*

As I approach Bethlehem, I pray the innkeeper will greet me. He'll show me how to use my imagination to help bring the love of Christ to others.

Mittens and books, blankets and stables won't reform the world. But they are candles in the darkness. Surely in this holy season, there must be some candle I can light, something I can do, for someone in need.

Free Meals
Hilda Sowers

FOR MANY YEARS Madaline Catt operated her own restaurant in Mishawaka, Indiana. Almost every day, two or three hitchhikers would stop for a free meal; no one was ever turned away.

Madaline would seat each one and hand him a menu, just as if he were a paying customer. An employee once asked why she didn't give the strangers something inexpensive to eat. She replied, "They might not like my choice."

The employee continued, "Well, why feed so many?"

Madaline's answer was simple: "I don't want to turn away anyone who is hungry, for the Master taught us:
what you do for others,
you do for
Him."

Prayer

Dear Lord! Kind Lord!
Gracious Lord! I pray
Thou wilt look on all I love,
Tenderly today!
Weed their hearts of weariness;
Scatter every care
Down a wake of angel-wings
Winnowing the air.

Bring unto the sorrowing
All release from pain;
Let the lips of laughter
Overflow again;
And with all the needy
O divide, I pray,
This vast measure of content
That is mine today!

—James Whitcomb Riley

PART 8

Transforming Power

Are you in an impossible situation? Try loving your way out of it! Love has the power to transform situations, other people — and even ourselves. Love can change the world! As the old rabbi put it, night ends and day begins when you can look at the face of a stranger and recognize that it is really the face of your brother.

Try Loving Your Way Out of the Kitchen

Helen Ferguson

WHEN I ARRIVED in New York at the age of sixteen, I expected all my dreams to come true.

I had $28 in my purse and a scrapbook of clippings which chronicled my budding career as a motion picture actress in Chicago. But my real equipment for success lay in my complete faith in the power of prayer; in my gratitude that I was an American. In America, my mother had taught me, one could earn anything one was willing to work hard for. I believed her.

Even in those days $28 was a little less than a fortune! Within six weeks my money was spent. My scrapbook was frayed from my eager displaying of it. I was homesick, my shoes needed resoling, and I was stranded in a brownstone front rooming-house in Brooklyn. But I wasn't scared. You can't be scared when your heart is filled with faith, your mind filled with prayer.

I had to have a roof over my head, so I made a deal with my landlady. She moved me into a dinky attic room, and for that heatless cubicle I agreed to do the daily clean-up work on all four floors of her multiple-tenanted house. I was to have afternoons off for my agency-haunting treks from Brooklyn to Manhattan. My meals I had to pay for by whatever babysitting job I could get at night.

I soon discovered my deep, stark hatred of the ugly kitchen. Despite my most energetic attentions, it always looked dreary. And I hated washing dishes. Passionately, I hated that endless, unrewarding task.

I was also filled with self-pity. A leading lady in Chicago, here I was washing dishes in an ugly house in Brooklyn, making no money to send home to my mother and sister.

Once there had been lots of money, the big house, servants, nursemaids, my beloved pony and cart. But that ended before I was four and the memory of it was blurred. My clear memories were of Mother sewing, sewing, sewing, trying to support me and my sister on what she could make as a dressmaker. Now, having dreamed of doing so much, I was scrubbing and cleaning. I was furious with resentment. I hated, even, every cup and saucer. I had to pay for each cup, saucer, plate or glass I broke. And I broke more each day.

It was hard to pray through all that hate and self-pity.

Sunday school was an oasis in my misery and bewilderment. It was like holding my mother's hand. And finally, what a blessing came from confiding my problem to my Sunday school teacher on a particular Sunday after breaking more dishes than usual. It wasn't easy to give this confidence. I was a proud young thing and it hurt to feel helpless.

"I just don't understand," I said flatly. "Why aren't my prayers answered?"

"Because you 'pray amiss,' Helen," she said gently. "You have been taught that Divine Love alone governs us, protects and directs us; that hatred never solved a problem nor dissolved an obstacle. Love, though, will do both."

"You mean I have to love that kitchen?"

"You don't have to love that kitchen, but you do have to love your way out of it. Unless, of course, you're happy hating it."

That loving rebuke brought the humble realization that I had been dictating to God, thereby not following my religious training at all.

It was a tall order, I thought, as I walked "home." But it had to be filled. I started being grateful that I had a place to live. And from that small gratefulness, the expense of replacing broken dishes stopped. Because — I stopped breaking them!

It didn't happen in the twinkling of an eye, but I found myself taking a pride in the *cleanliness* of the kitchen. Then, in the *neatness* of its shelves. I bought some bright paper and was delighted at the *happy* look of those shelves. Under this enthusiasm I spent a hard-earned dollar on bright calico, and then I persuaded the landlady to make perkily ruffled curtains. I coaxed a discouraged geranium bud to grow into an ambitious red bloom in a pot around which I'd wrapped a bit of crisp crepe paper.

And I was so proud and happy with my production!

I don't know, nor can I ever remember, just when hate left. Suddenly all was lovely, and the hate was gone. The landlady never thanked me, but one night I discovered a new pillow case on my bed. At the store one day I learned she'd invited the neighbors in to view the kitchen and had said, "The child will go where she wants. Work don't scare that one."

In a burst of gratitude I rushed to the dime store and bought a half-dozen sparkling new glasses as a gift for *my* kitchen. When I reached it there was a message. My first call from the Edward Small Agency!

My work was done in that house. I had literally and spiritually loved my way out of it. I had gained a positive, scientific rule for overcoming anything that could overwhelm me.

There is really no end to my kitchen story. Its principle is ever-present in my business and social life, and proving that principle — over and over — is one of life's continuing adventures. I wish I could say I always prove it instantly and unfailingly. I would feel far more deserving if I could say that.

The warfare with oneself is not fought in a sparkling arena, but in some murky corner of consciousness which, when one has loved enough, becomes bright and gay and peaceful because love glows there.

My picture career climbed steadily, carrying me from New York to Hollywood. The things I dreamed of doing came into existence whenever I demonstrated the scientific power of prayer.

When my first husband passed away, I retired permanently from the screen, and two years later married again. In 1932, at the nadir of a depression, my husband's bank closed; he was completely broken in the crash. Thus came the opportunity for me to prove whether I had grown in my understanding of the lesson I had learned at sixteen.

Could I now, with four step-children to support, resist resentment, disappointment and fear of the future and rely unquestioningly on Divine Love to meet my every human need?

I wasn't sixteen this time — and I *was* scared. Until I took stock on a comparative basis. I wasn't sixteen, but I was wiser. And most important of all, I had the proved and tested equipment for success: faith in prayer, gratitude that I was an American, and I still believed what Mother had taught me — one could earn anything one was willing to work hard for.

In 1933, in the fogs of depression, with no one, humanly, to back me, I started in business: Helen Ferguson, Publicity.

During my years as an actress I had always felt there was a need to raise the accepted level of Hollywood publicity — a need to picture most of its citizenry accurately.

I called or wrote dozens of prospective clients. I heard from none of them. I sat in my tiny $15-a-month office and waited. Nobody came. It could have been like my first weeks in my landlady's kitchen so long ago except . . . this time I already knew the principle to be proved. If I was about my Father's business, doing whatever was at hand with love, my human needs would be met.

Then days later lovely Faye Wray became my first client. Three months later I moved to a larger office, and four months after that had my own building with four offices. My husband passed on eleven years ago. I have eight offices today*; clients who are also my friends; my step-children are all grown and married. Mother and I share a spacious home.

It *is* a success story. I know that. I am humbly grateful for my participation in it, but it is not a *personal* success story. It is the story of the success of a principle, a principle available to all.

Every day I remember the words of my Sunday school teacher, "Never for an instant stop loving — for in that you deny your identification with Him — reject His power to help you. Never circumscribe

---

*Written in 1953.

God by outlining what action He shall take. Take your actions carefully, fearlessly, lovingly, and trust God to bring about the right result."

When, as too often happens, anything less is recorded in my experience, it is because I have, for that space of time, failed in my obedience — forgotten, if ever so briefly, the story of my kitchen.

The Unexpected Weapon
Constance Foster

MY FRIEND, May Haviland, was a middle-aged Quaker with a ramrod bearing and the softest brown eyes in the world. Quaker ancestors had suffered persecution in early America rather than compromise with their principles. One of them was nonresistance and it was bred into May Haviland's bones.

The Havilands were a well-to-do old family, and May was the last of a long line of them. She lived unostentatiously in Brooklyn but made at least one trip abroad every year. Paris was her favorite destination and she stayed always at the same modest pension where her habits were like clockwork. It was well known, too, that she brought with her the family jewels inherited from a succession of aunts and cousins.

One evening she came down to dinner intending to spend her usual hour or two in the lobby reading newspapers. But this night she discovered that she had forgotten her handkerchief, so after the meal she went back to her room for it.

As May opened her door, she was astounded to see a burly, dark-haired man rifling her bureau drawers. Quietly May closed the door behind her and at the faint click the burglar whirled, a revolver in his hand.

"If there's one thing I dislike," she told the intruder firmly, "it's guns. Please put that thing down. I am not going to call for the police. I am going to help you because you must need whatever I have much more than I do, if you have to steal for it."

The burglar was utterly dumbfounded when May opened the secret drawer of a small rosewood desk where her rings were hidden. She talked to him quietly, reassuringly, pressing the jewelry on him and telling him that she was sorry for him since his need was so urgent.

Suddenly the man dropped his gun to the floor, let out a low cry and fled, taking nothing.

The following day there was an unsigned note in May's mailbox. It read: "Madam, I have known only hate and fear. I can deal with them. But I was powerless before your kindness."

May told me the story later.

"Even guns," she said, "are

silent in the face

of love."

She Had the Answer
Carl E. Calkins
as told to Thomas W. Calkins

THE WAYS OF A WOMAN are strange — but often rather wonderful. Take my wife, Luetta. She worked from sunrise to sunset, for life on our farm was hard. Yet she never complained.

I knew she was very religious — just like my mother. When we were first married, Luetta came back from visiting her one day and said, "Your mother has something, Carl; she lives her religion."

Then Mother died. And soon after the funeral, Luetta told me that she had taken her stand for the Lord. But I wasn't ready for religion.

Our homestead was on the prairie and it was wonderful to think of building something from nothing. But working from sunrise to sunset was hard. I'd hitch up the sixteen horses, plow and harrow in the spring, and plant in the fall. But year after year something happened and there would be a crop failure. By then we had two boys. And I'd feel tired just realizing that we had little to show for months of dirt and sweat.

But Luetta bore me up through it all. Funny though, she never said much to me about her God. She would just help me nail the shingles on our three-room shack and hum while she hammered. She would tend the chickens and milk the cows. She would bake bread, the aroma of which practically drew me in from the fields.

I remember one night I went to bed but couldn't get to sleep. Luetta didn't come right away. The kitchen was off to one side so I could see the light in there through the crack in the door. I got up and stood at the kitchen door in my nightshirt and bare feet and watched Luetta.

She had her Bible open on the table. And after a spell she knelt right down on the plank floor. I couldn't hear her much but I could see her lips moving in prayer.

It dawned on me, then and there, how truly important was the faith that kept Luetta steady.

A short time later I took the Lord into my own life. After I had, I asked Luetta why she had never tried to convert me.

I'll never forget her answer; she just pushed back a wisp of hair and smiled kind of wistful from where she stood by the pump at the water cistern.

"I did," she said. "I loved you into the church."

In One Blinding Moment
Max Ellerbusch

IT WAS A BUSY FRIDAY, six days before Christmas, 1958. I was in my instrument-repair shop here in Cincinnati, Ohio, working feverishly so that I could have all of the Christmas holiday at home with my family. Then the phone rang and a voice was saying that our five-year-old Craig had been hit by a car.

There was a crowd standing around him by the time I got there, but they stepped back for me. Craig was lying in the middle of the road; his curly blond hair was not even rumpled.

He died at Children's Hospital that afternoon.

There were many witnesses. It had happened at the school crossing. They told us that Craig had waited on the curb until the safety-patrol boy signaled him to cross. Craig, how well you remembered! How often your mother called after you as you started off for kindergarten, "Don't cross till you get the signal!" You didn't forget!

The signal came, Craig stepped into the street. The car came so fast no one had seen it. The patrol boy shouted, waved, had to jump for his own life. The car never stopped.

Grace and I drove home from the hospital through the Christmas-lighted streets, not believing what had happened to us. It wasn't until night, passing the unused bed, that I knew. Suddenly I was crying, not just for that empty bed but for the emptiness, the senselessness of life itself. All night long, with Grace awake beside me, I searched what I knew of life for some hint of a loving God at work in it, and found none.

As a child I certainly had been led to expect none. My father used to say that in all his childhood he did not experience one act of charity or Christian kindness. Father was an orphan, growing up in nineteenth-century Germany, a supposedly Christian land. Orphans were rented out to farmers as machines are rented today, and treated with far less consideration. He grew into a stern, brooding man who looked upon life as an unassisted journey to the grave.

He married another orphan and, as their own children started to come, they decided to emigrate to America. Father got a job aboard a ship; in New York harbor he went ashore and simply kept going. He stopped in Cincinnati where so many Germans were then settling. He took every job he could find, and in a year and a half had saved enough money to send for his family.

On the boat coming over, two of my sisters contracted scarlet fever; they died on Ellis Island. Something in Mother died with them, for from that day on she showed no affection for any living being. I grew up in a silent house, without laughter, without faith.

Later, in my own married life, I was determined not to allow these grim shadows to fall on our own children. Grace and I had four: Diane, Michael, Craig and Ruth Carol. It was Craig, even more than the others, who seemed to lay low my childhood pessimism, to tell me that the world was a wonderful and purposeful place. As a baby he would smile so delightedly at everyone he saw that there was always a little group around his carriage. When we went visiting it was Craig, three years old, who would run to the hostess to say, "You have a lovely house!" If he received a gift he was touched to tears, and then gave it away to the first child who envied it. Sunday morning when Grace dressed to sing in the choir, it was Craig who never forgot to say, "You're beautiful."

And if such a child can die, I thought as I fought my bed that Friday night, if such a life can be snuffed out in a minute, then life is meaningless and faith in God is self-delusion. By morning my hopelessness and helplessness had found a target, a blinding hatred for the person who had done this to us. That morning police picked him up in Tennessee: George Williams.* Fifteen years old.

He came from a broken home, police learned. His mother worked a night shift and slept during the day. Friday he had cut school, taken her car keys while she was asleep, sped down a street . . . All my rage at a senseless universe seemed to focus on the name George Williams. I phoned our lawyer and begged him to prosecute Williams to the limit. "Get him tried as an adult, juvenile court's not tough enough."

So this was my frame of mind when the thing occurred which changed my life. I cannot explain it, I can only describe it.

It happened in the space of time that it takes to walk two steps. It was late Saturday night. I was pacing the hall outside our bedroom, my head in my hands. I felt sick and dizzy, and tired, so tired. "O God," I prayed, "show me why!"

Right then, between that step and the next, my life was changed. The breath went out of me in a great sigh—and with it all the

---

*At the Ellerbusches' request George's real name is not used.

sickness. In its place was a feeling of love and joy so strong it was almost pain.

Others have called it "the presence of Christ." I'd known the phrase, of course, but I'd thought it was some abstract, theological idea. I never dreamed it was Someone, an actual Person, filling that narrow hall with love.

It was the suddenness of it that dazed me. It was like a lightning stroke that turned out to be the dawn. I stood blinking in an unfamiliar light. Vengefulness, grief, hate, anger — it was not that I struggled to be rid of them — like goblins imagined in the dark, in morning's light they simply were not there.

And all the while I had the extraordinary feeling that I was two people. I had another self, a self that was millions of miles from that hall, learning things men don't yet have words to express. I have tried so often to remember the things I knew then, but the learning seemed to take place in a mind apart from the one I ordinarily think with, as though the answer to my question was too vast for my small intellect. But, in that mind beyond logic, that question was answered. In that instant I *knew* why Craig had to leave us. Though I had no visual sensation, I knew afterward that I had met him, and that he was wiser than I, so that I was the little boy and he the man. And he was so busy. Craig had so much to do, unimaginably important things into which I must not inquire. My concerns were still on earth.

In the clarity of that moment it came to me: this life is a simple thing! I remember the very words in which the thought came. "Life is a grade in school; in this grade we must learn only one lesson: we must establish relationships of love."

Oh, Craig, I thought. *Little Craig, in your five short years how fast you learned, how quickly you progressed, how soon you graduated!*

I don't know how long I stood there in the hall. Perhaps it was no time at all as we ordinarily measure things. Grace was sitting up in bed when I reached the door of our room. Not reading, not doing anything, just looking straight ahead of her as she had much of the time since Friday afternoon.

Even my appearance must have changed because as she turned her eyes slowly to me she gave a little gasp and sat up straighter. I started to talk, words rumbling over each other, laughing, eager, trying to say that the world was not an accident, that life meant something, that earthly tragedy was not the end, that all around our incompleteness was a universe of purpose, that the purpose was good beyond our furthest hopes.

"Tonight," I told her, "Craig is beyond needing us. Someone else needs us. George Williams. It's almost Christmas. Maybe, at the Juvenile Detention Home, there'll be no Christmas gift for him unless we send it."

Grace listened, silent, unmoving, staring at me. Suddenly she burst into tears.

"Yes," she said. "That's right, that's right. It's the first thing that's been right since Craig died."

And it has been right. George turned out to be an intelligent, confused, desperately lonely boy, needing a father as much as I needed a son. He got his gift, Christmas Day, and his mother got a box of Grace's good Christmas cookies. We asked for and got his release, a few days later, and this house became his second home. He works with me in the shop after school, joins us for meals around the kitchen table, is a big brother for Diane and Michael and Ruth Carol.

But more was changed, in that moment when I met Christ, than just my feeling about George. That meeting has affected every phase of my life, my approach to business, to friends, to strangers. I don't mean I've been able to sustain the ecstacy of that moment; I doubt that the human body could contain such joy for very many days.

But I now know with infinite sureness that no matter what life
does to us in the future, I will never again touch the
rock-bottom of despair. No matter how ultimate
the blow seems, I glimpsed an even
more ultimate joy in that
blinding moment
when the door
swung wide.

Love Is Contagious
Amy Washburn

ALICE WAS PAST RETIREMENT AGE for teachers, but it was her nature to fight against all rules, so it did not surprise us that she continued at her desk. She had always been outspoken and defiant.

The little clique of teachers of which I was part ignored her most of the time. We tried to stay out of range of her stinging temper and sarcastic tongue.

It is understandable that we were quite upset when she was named principal of the school during mid-term, replacing a woman who resigned because of illness.

The wrath of the new regime was felt immediately. Alice shouted commands and even berated us in front of our classes. She was harsh with the children too. Finally, we mutinied and went as a group to the superintendent.

He laughed off our charges saying, "No one can be that bad."

The following day, three of us were eating in the lunchroom when Alice — flushed with rage — marched to our table and accused us of talking about her. As she left, I suddenly felt sympathetic toward her. For the first time, I saw her as she really was — a pitiful, lonesome, old lady who needed our prayers instead of our censure.

I told the others and they agreed we should pray for her as well as ourselves, that we might gain a better understanding.

Slowly at first, we drew her into our circle. We remembered her birthday with little gifts. We invited her to eat with us. She who had been a stranger gradually blossomed into a warm human being.

We learned that her sister's husband had been ill, and it was Alice's paycheck that kept the family going. Her small niece had needed surgery for a heart condition, and Alice volunteered her savings for the operation. It became very clear why Alice's clothing was outdated and worn. Now we understood why she had worked past retirement age.

The miracle was the change that took place. Bit by bit, our love expressed in simple terms was reflected by her kindness. Love is contagious. Now our school is a better place.

I have heard the Sermon on the Mount many times, but it
took Alice to teach me what Christ was talking about
when He said, "Love your enemies, bless
them that curse you, do good to them
that hate you, and pray for
them which despitefully
use you . . . " (Matthew
5:44).Even teachers
need to go back
to school
some-
times.

So Much to Love
Mary L. Holmes

OUR FAMILY HAD BEEN EXPERIENCING a "winter of discontent." We had totaled up five weeks of mumps, one case of measles, a broken leg, a broken nose and the emergence of four stubborn new teeth for the baby. Through it all I had managed to maintain my equanimity. But one evening, after a particularly trying day, my resources ran dry.

The baby had gone to bed howling, the broken nose was in need of a hot compress, the victim of the broken leg was awaiting help with his bath, and my mumpsy husband was hopefully calling for a Pinochle partner. By some miracle the living room was empty and I threw myself down on the couch, burying my head on my knees. "O Lord, I have so much to do!" was my intended cry. To my astonishment, what I said in fact was, "O Lord, I have so much to love!"

After a moment's meditation, I arose and tackled my duties
with new-found strength and cheerfulness.
Surely God had a hand in
this slip of the
heart!

I Didn't Want to Be
a Grandfather
*Will Gorman**

A FEW YEARS AGO my thirty-year-old daughter picked the night of the Dodger playoff game to tell me she was pregnant — hoping I'd be so enthralled with the game that I wouldn't be too upset by the news. She had tested my nervous system just a few weeks earlier by revealing that her husband had decided to strap his guitar to his motorcycle, file for divorce and head for new frontiers.

He had the charm of a giraffe with a bad cough, so I wasn't really that sad to see him leave. But now she told me that one reason he had bailed out of the marriage was the fact that she was pregnant, and he wanted nothing whatever to do with becoming a father.

Pregnant? I was more than upset. I was angry.

My life has been slightly rocky since my wife died, at the age of twenty-three, leaving me with a three-year-old daughter. Even though little Ellen has always been a joy to me, she has also been testing my patience for twenty-seven years.

Now I was suddenly very tired of parental responsibility. I was tired of protecting, of being concerned, of arguing. I was tired of the constant drain on my wallet, and I was tired of telling myself, "She doesn't mean to be a pain in the neck. Under all this oddness is a good kid."

---

*All names have been changed.

She's the type who refused to study in high school. "Dad, there's more to life than being a secretary. I want to do something outdoors!" My first gray hair sprang from my skull when she announced that her life's goal was to become a bicycle mechanic at Yosemite.

For the previous ten years she had been like a sack of firecrackers, popping off noisily every time I relaxed. I had learned to accept her selfish and silly way of living. But pregnancy was an entirely different matter. I knew there was only one thing to do.

"I'll make arrangements to have this taken care of," I said.

Ellen had always done an excellent job of ignoring my advice — usually reacting with fury and fight — but now she was just smiling at me.

"No, Dad. I'm going to have this baby. I didn't plan for things to be like this, but I'm going to be a mother!"

I looked at that new smile, and heard the words, and should have realized I was suddenly dealing with a woman, not with the rebellious teenager who had never quite grown up.

I marshaled all my facts and warnings and shot them at her as fast as I could. *Bang:* You have no husband! *Bang:* You have no job! *Bang:* You have no education! *Bang:* You have no savings! *Bang, bang, bang:* You have nothing, nothing, nothing! And now you're going to put the cap on your life by bringing a baby into it.

"I refuse to pick up after you anymore," I shouted. "You are *not* going to mess up another person's life with your selfishness. You are not going to have that baby!"

Still smiling, she stood up and headed for the door. "I'm sorry about all this, Dad. But I will not have an abortion." She opened the door to leave.

"Just what do you think you're going to *do*?" I yelled.

"God'll take care of me," she said as she got into her car and drove away.

That bit of news surprised me just as much as the news of the pregnancy.

God? "God will take care of me?" What did she mean by that?

During her formative years I had made sure that she had not fallen under the influence of any religion. I told her it was foolishness that would turn her brain to pudding, and she had always agreed with my counsel — or I thought she had. God, indeed!

I was too mad to talk for a week or so, but when I became calmer and a wee bit more rational, I phoned her — and gently told her that it was unwise to continue her pregnancy.

And she calmly told me that she was going to have her baby.

During the next few weeks we tiptoed around each other, softly fencing for position. I'd tell her how difficult her life was going to be as a single mother, and she'd tell me she was going to have her baby. She never wavered.

It was a full month before I realized that I was facing a new person — a steadfast, determined and stubborn person who was going to become a mother!

"Okay, okay," I said, finally giving up the idea of an abortion. "But what was that stuff about being helped by 'God'?"

"I knew you'd be mad when I told you I was pregnant," she said. "So I went to a church and talked to the minister about my problem. The church has a Crisis Pregnancy Center and he sent me there."

So by the time she had approached me with the news, she had been counseled by a group of churchwomen — some of whom had had abortions, and some who had had their babies when an abortion would have been an easy way out. And while seeking answers, Ellen had found her God.

"I'll make a deal with you," I said. "I'll accept the idea of your being a mother — but don't ever, ever try to talk me into going to church!"

She just smiled again.

Ellen had one final challenge for my sanity. She announced that she was going to have her baby in her apartment, with only the assistance of a midwife.

"Call me when all this foolishness is over," I snapped.

During the following months I watched as she became more and more involved with her church and her pending motherhood. And the more she bloomed, the more I withered.

I knew she'd have to move out of her apartment when the child was born. In fact, I knew she'd have to move in with me! I resented the fact that she had refused to take my advice and had forced me into a position where I had no choice but to take on a new and heavy burden just at a time in life when I was getting ready to lay parts of the old load aside.

If "God" was going to take care of all these new problems, why did I feel so trapped?

Then, one afternoon while I was at my office, the phone rang. Ellen's breathless voice was filled with a joy I had never heard before. "Your grandson is here! Hurry over. He'll be ready to meet you in twenty minutes!"

I drove the ten miles to her apartment and walked in, wondering what life had in store for me now.

She was standing at the door waiting for me, with "six pounds of sleepy" in her arms.

She handed him to me—and my life changed.

The first time I touched little Will's cheek and held his tiny hand, things began to fall apart inside me. If I had been listening, I'm sure I could have heard the sounds of anger crumbling, of teeth unclenching, of frown lines disintegrating—and when he gave forth a loud yawn, I knew the meaning of "making a joyful noise."

Within a week I had moved Ellen and her son to my house, and then this special little messenger began to mend my heart, soul and mind. And he did the same for his testy, grouchy mother, who became more and more involved with her church, and easier and easier to be around.

During the following months, I often sat holding his hand while I watched him sleep, and I was filled with dreams and hopes that had been absent for decades. He filled my hours with wonder. The only nervousness I ever felt was when Ellen took him off to church with her several times a week. But I kept my mouth shut. In the past I would have warned her of the myth of religion—but something stopped the words.

During his second year I taught him to walk and how to go to the bathroom, and he started stringing words together to express his interest in all these new things around him. We discussed bugs and grass and wind. We investigated dew and reflections in rain puddles. Together we eagerly checked the sky each night to see if the moon had returned, and together we sat in a dark room, holding a flashlight against the bottom of my hand so he could investigate my bones.

Shortly after his most recent birthday—his third—I introduced him to the goofiness of special Friday night "stags." While his mom went out, we stayed home to eat "banilla" ice cream smothered in chocolate sauce and watch reruns of the Three Stooges.

He always talks to the dogs and cats when we go for our nightly walk around the block. He hums Rossini sonatas while entertaining his rubber duck in the bathtub. He sings right along with Lionel Richie. He says dandelions need a shave.

One day recently we were strolling through the aisles at the supermarket. As usual he was standing up in the cart, making various purchasing recommendations, when he started to sing one of his little church songs—something about God being very nice.

"So you think God's pretty neat, huh?" I asked.

"Sure," he said, pointing to a shelf. "He made me just for you. There's the chocolate stuff right there."

I was stunned. *He made me just for you.* The words echoed through my mind like the sound of a beautiful bell. I suddenly remembered all the anger I felt at the news of his arrival. I remembered Ellen smiling as I ranted. I remembered her saying, "God will take care of me."

I thank Ellen for ignoring my advice. I thank little Will for giving me joy and love I never knew before. And I thank God for taking care of all of us.

When Darkness Ends
Sue Monk Kidd

IN SUNDAY SCHOOL one morning we launched into a discussion of how much darkness there was in the world. War, hunger, hate, homelessness. "When will it end?" a woman asked.

Her question reminded me of the rabbi who asked his students a question. "When does night end and day begin?"

One student asked, "Is it the moment you're able to perceive the difference between an olive tree and a fig tree?"

"No," said the rabbi. "That's not it."

"Is it the moment you can tell the difference between a sheep and a dog?" asked another.

The rabbi shook his head. "No, that's not it either. Rather it is the moment you look at the face of a stranger and recognize that it is really the face of your brother."

Perhaps that *is* when night ends in our world and day begins.

Today, if I practice seeing the strangers who come my way as
brothers and sisters, I might find a new attitude
dawning in my life. And maybe there will be
even a bit more light in
the world.

PART 9

The Circle of Love

Love given is never wasted. It continues to grow and multiply. When we receive a kindness or a loving gift, we may not be able to repay the giver. But we create the circle by passing on the kindness to someone else. When we reach out to others in their time of need, we help create a ring of love that supports them and keeps them from falling. And sometimes, in God's mysterious ways, we see the two ends of the circle meet.

Richer Than Kings
Fred Bauer

RIGHT NOW, at this very moment, more than a few faithful Christians are carrying enormous burdens. Hurt, worried, fearful, depressed, lonely, bereaved, sick, and defeated would only partially describe their myriad problems. But I know that there is something that can help ease that suffering. It is the realization that we are all part of a circle of love that can uphold us even in our most trying times.

No matter how poor in spirit you feel today, you won't sink if you hold onto that life-preserving ring. You can, in fact, count yourself richer than kings . . .

> If you have someone to *love* . . .
> If someone requites your *love* . . .
> If living alone, with *love* to give, you seek another, your *love* to bestow . . .
> If you have a job or endeavor that you *love* to do . . .
> If you know that despite any failure, shortcoming or mistake, you have a forgiving heavenly Father who *loves* you more than any *love* you can imagine.

That's the Good News
today.

The Secret of
Receiving a Gift
Martha S. Foster

T HE DOORBELL of my two-room furnished apartment rang one morning shortly after my husband and I moved to Columbus, Ohio. We knew no one in the entire city, and as I lumbered across the room—I was expecting my first baby—I said to myself, "If it's a salesman, he's wasting his time."

After four years of medical school—on borrowed money—we could not even afford those things we needed. Our baby's layette consisted of two or three blankets, a few diapers and a couple of shirts. Every day to save bus fare my husband walked to the hospital.

I opened the front door. A short, middle-aged woman with friendly blue eyes stood in the hallway smiling at me. She carried nothing but a drawstring bag the color of her eyes.

"Good morning," she said. "I'm Lorena Blackmore. I knew your mother."

Then she walked back to a battered car parked at the curb, returning with a carton piled high with baby clothes.

"My kids have outgrown these," she said. "I want you to have them — I think that's what I've been saving them for."

I was overjoyed. "How can I ever repay you?" I asked.

Lorena smiled. "I'm too old for babies anymore so you can't return the clothes to me. You can pay me the interest on the loan but the principal you can only pay to someone else, when you have it."

"I don't understand," I said. Principal and interest sounded so businesslike to me. For a moment, I was suspicious.

Lorena sat down on the couch, opened the blue bag and took out her knitting. "I figured out the idea when William and I were married," she explained. "William was still going to school and I worked in an office. We had no car and no way to get out of the city. I was a country girl and was lonely for the fields and trees. Then my boss's wife began taking me in her limousine to a farm they owned. No one but me will ever know how much those rides meant. I felt I could never repay Mrs. Leslie for them and I couldn't; not in the same way or degree.

"It was easy for me to do something in return to pay the interest, however — baby-sit or wash the dishes when she entertained — but the original debt could be repaid in full only to someone else."

"How could you ever return the car rides?" I asked.

"That came later. When William and I were able to buy an old car, I found a shut-in who lived nearby. She enjoyed the rides we took each Thursday to the Olentangy Woods.

"But that was only one debt," she continued. "We accumulate a great many during a lifetime. When I was a little girl, a neighbor let me come into her house anytime I wished to play her Victrola. Through her I discovered a whole world of beauty. I still have that debt to repay to some other child."

Lorena's system intrigued me, especially when she told me that it worked backward as well as forward. You sometimes give because of what you never received, but needed. So it was with her husband.

"When William was fourteen," she said, "his father was very ill in the hospital. That summer a couple of William's friends and their fathers went on a canoe trip into Canada. William would have given anything in the world to go on that canoe trip. But they didn't ask him. And because they didn't, William has since taken seven canoe trips, each with a different boy — a boy lonesome for a father he doesn't have.

"So you repay the kindness you don't get, as well as the kindness you do get," she explained. "Maybe that's what I'm doing right now. You see, by the time William and I paid for the car and had Tom, there was no money for baby clothes."

I stared at a soft, cotton-flannel nightgown with drawstring cuffs that had toppled from the carton to the floor. The little nightgown seemed to me the most beautiful nightgown I had ever seen.

"But how do you know what to give — and to whom?" I asked.

"All you need is a good memory," Lorena answered.

But I knew you needed more — you needed a loving heart like Lorena's that knew no limitations.

Since that day I have often thought of Lorena's practice of giving. Her words, "All you need is a good memory," have helped me become aware of the many helping hands which have stretched out to me.

Through Lorena I learned that it is never too late to return such gifts.

And I learned that finding the right person and the
right moment adds zest to what
is a real adventure
in giving.

Others

It doesn't matter who you are,
Or what you have, or do.
If you give of your very best
The best returns to you.
A law of compensation works,
We get just what we earn,
If we love others with our hearts,
We get love in return.
The little things we sometimes do
For others day by day,
Return quite unexpectedly
In some peculiar way.

— Herbert Parker

No Room to Fall
B. J. Connor

I ONCE HEARD the mother of a teenage boy who was paralyzed in an accident explain how she kept from having a breakdown herself:

"Our church friends formed a circle around us so tightly, there was no room to fall."

I love her description. Can't you just picture people holding hands, surrounding that devastated huddle of a family like children playing "Farmer in the Dell"? Of course, they didn't literally encompass them. But they surrounded them with love. They sent cards and letters of encouragement, brought meals, built a wheelchair ramp, chipped in money for expenses, helped modify the house, visited with jokes and news and tutoring and prayed, and other unnamed kindnesses, all of which helped pull the family through a difficult time.

What a privilege to be fellow participants in this game called "Bearing One Another's Burdens." Because sometimes we're one of the strong ones forming the circle. And sometimes we're one of the broken ones inside.

A Kindness Returned
Esther Ueberall

IT WAS A Friday morning in December 1902, our first day of business. I was a seventeen-year-old newlywed standing by my husband, Solomon, in our little notions shop on Myrtle Avenue in Brooklyn. We had poured all our money and hopes into Ueberall's 3-9-19-cents store.

Standing before us now was our first customer. He was the young priest, Father Caruana, of a little storefront Catholic church.

As he paid my husband, his face was as somber as his suit.

"Why so sad, Father?" Solomon asked. He was the kind who was touched by another's sorrow.

"Oh," answered the priest absentmindedly, "the little store building where we're worshiping is about to be closed."

"But why?" pressed my husband. To him religion was an every-hour devotion. Touching the mezuzah at the door of our room above the store was not a habit but an opportunity to acknowledge the Lord.

The priest explained that unless he could raise $500 by Monday morning, the mortgage on his building would be foreclosed. Since his was a poor parish, there was no likelihood of raising the money. It seemed he didn't want to arrange a loan through his chancery office. We also got the impression he thought the authorities might veto his plans for a church here.

As my husband listened to the priest's troubled words, his hand gripped my arm. I sensed his inner feelings. Both of us were Jewish immigrants—my husband from Austria, I from Russia. Each of our families sought sanctuary here from persecution in Europe. We remembered the pogroms in which men broke into homes at night to carry loved ones away.

"No, no," Solomon was saying. "That cannot be." The thought that a church must be closed for lack of money was abhorrent. Here in America, of all places, a house of worship must be safe.

My husband put his hand on the priest's shoulder. "Don't worry, Father," he said. "We'll get the money for you somehow." I was astounded; we didn't even have five dollars cash.

Father Caruana stared at my husband. Then, unable to believe what he had heard, he shook his head and slowly walked out.

Solomon turned to me. "Esther, you know all those wedding presents we got? I'm going to pawn them. Someday we'll get them back, but right now we have to raise that five hundred dollars."

Already he was unfastening the watch and chain my father had given him. He looked down at my engagement ring. I slowly worked it off and handed it to him.

But that afternoon when Solomon returned from the pawn broker, he was downcast. He could get only $250 for the gifts. Later, as we ate supper, he exclaimed, "I know! We have a big family. We can borrow from them."

All day Sunday, Solomon went from uncle to brother-in-law, from cousin to nephew, many of whom he had helped before. Some were sympathetic, some reluctant. Solomon argued. He pleaded. He exhorted. Finally, in bits here and pieces there, he obtained the additional $250.

Each Monday from then on, Father Caruana was the first visitor to our store. With him he brought a leather pouch full of change collected from his parishioners. Our friendship deepened. And finally the day arrived when the last cent was paid off.

Meanwhile I was again wearing my ring and we had our gifts back. Prosperity smiled on our shop and it became Ueberall's Department Store. As it grew, so did Father Caruana's storefront congregation, until one day the diocese decided to build a large church called St. Lucy's. Solomon watched its construction with fascination.

"Look, Esther," he would exclaim, coming back into the store. "Now they are putting the door lintels on."

Through the years the department store was like another parish house; we would provide merchandise for church bazaars, booths and other functions. Then, in 1919, Father Caruana was called to Rome. He and Solomon parted like saddened brothers.

The following year tragedy struck when Solomon suddenly died from a heart attack. So terrible was my shock that I lost my eyesight for almost two years. When it returned, I devoted myself to running the store and raising my two children, Bernard and Stella.

Years passed. I became busy in civic affairs and the Red Cross. Now Bernie managed the store. Gradually the memory of Father Caruana faded from my mind.

Then World War II broke out. Hitler marched into Austria. And again there were pogroms.

Soon letters began to pack my mailbox—letters from Solomon's relatives and former townsmen in Austria, begging me to help them reach America and escape the death camps. I helped as many as I could, getting them visas to enter America. But soon immigration quotas were filled.

The letters kept coming. Each was like a knife stabbing my heart. I would lean on the pile and cry, "Oh, Solomon, I know if you were here you would help me."

Finally I went to the Labor Department in Washington, D.C. They told me that refugees could still find sanctuary in Cuba if some prominent person there would sign affidavits vouching for them.

What to do? I knew no one in Cuba. Then it occurred to me: Cuba was a Catholic country, so I went to St. Lucy's. A young priest there gave me a letter of introduction to the papal nuncio in Cuba. He also cabled that I was coming.

Two days later my plane landed at the Havana airport. As I stepped down from the plane, a boy handed me a bouquet of roses. Looking up, I saw a red-robed man waiting behind him. He was smiling at me.

I was puzzled. There was something about his gentle brown eyes that seemed to go back through the years.

He held his arms out to me. "Esther Ueberall," he cried, "don't you remember me?"

It was Father Caruana!

I collapsed in tears. After we got into his car, he explained that since his assignment in Rome, he had become an archbishop and papal nuncio in Cuba.

With Father Caruana's help, more than two dozen family members escaped Hitler and reached Cuba. While they waited for U.S. Immigration quotas to reopen, they were not permitted to work. However, the archbishop not only sheltered them but also supplied them with clothing and food, including vegetables from his own garden and meats from a kosher market. In six months they were making new lives in America.

From then on Father Caruana and I kept in touch. Some years later he became ill and was sent to Misericordia Hospital in Philadelphia. I did not know this until I opened a letter from the mother superior: "His condition prevents him from seeing anyone, but he calls for you."

In three hours I was at his bedside. He looked so thin and pitiful against the white hospital sheets.

"Esther," he said, reaching for my hand.

We sat there, saying little. I knew he was preparing for a long journey.

After a while he said, "Esther, keep well. I pray for you and your dear family every day."

Then, with difficulty, he reached for something under his pillow, something that he obviously treasured. He pressed it into my hand. It was a tiny silver case containing a relic of St. Francis de Sales, a bit of his velvet robe.

"Keep this, Esther. It will remind you of a great saint."

Hot tears stung my eyes and I clung to his hand. I couldn't speak. But in my heart I cried, *Dear Father Caruana, you have already done this for me. For in your life I have seen God, and that will sustain me all the rest of my years.*

Part of the Circle
Dina Donohue

INDIA ALBERY WAS, perhaps, the most unusual person ever to work at Guideposts. Lady Albery—for that was her title—seldom spoke about herself. We knew only that she had come from England, that her early life had been privileged, but that when she first came to Guideposts, she was old and alone and impoverished, living in a shabby room with a few cherished keepsakes.

She met adversity bravely, but with a stern and haughty demeanor. I myself tried hard, but I could not break through her British reserve. I used to pray that I'd find some way to reach her, but she was too proud to let any emotion show.

One lunch hour in December, I was browsing in an antique shop, a favorite pastime. I seldom purchased anything, but this day was different. I spied an enamel pencil in a silver case. It had a large "A" in its elaborate monogram and I felt an urging—almost a physical nudge—to buy it for Lady Albery.

"What's this?" she asked brusquely when I handed her the tiny package.

"Just a little Christmas something," I said apprehensively.

When Lady Albery opened the package and saw the silver case, her body tensed, and her eyes filled with tears. "Dina," she said—never before had she used my first name—"Dina, how did you know?"

"Know what?" I asked.

"This once belonged to me," she said. "I had to sell it years ago, when
I was hungry and desperate. It was given to me by someone I
loved. And now your kindness has brought it back."
A circle of love, I thought, *I've been*
part of a circle of love.
And Lady Albery
never forgot
it.

The Gift of Love
was created by the same people
who publish *Guideposts*, a monthly magazine
filled with true stories of people's adventures in faith.
If you have enjoyed this book, we think you'll find help and
inspiration in the exciting stories that appear in our magazine.
Guideposts is not sold on the newsstand. It's available by
subscription only. And subscribing is easy.
All you have to do is write
Guideposts Associates, Inc.
39 Seminary Hill Road
Carmel, New York, 10512

For those with special reading needs, *Guideposts* is
published in Big Print, Braille, and Talking Magazine.
At the same time, you might in interested in ordering the
current volume of *Daily Guideposts*, an annual volume
of devotionals for each day of the year. Many of
the stories in *The Gift of Love* appeared
first in past volumes of
Daily Guideposts.